COLUMBIA UNIVERSITY ORIENTAL STUDIES
Vol. XXVIII

THE ORIGINS OF THE DRUZE PEOPLE AND RELIGION

WITH EXTRACTS FROM THEIR SACRED WRITINGS

BY

PHILIP K. HITTI, PH.D.
OF PRINCETON UNIVERSITY
FORMERLY OF THE AMERICAN UNIVERSITY OF BEIRUT

New York
COLUMBIA UNIVERSITY PRESS
1928

PLATE I.

Photostatic reproduction of the first page of Bahā'-al-Dīn's *al-Juz' al-Awwal*, one of the most valuable Druze sacred books by the father of Druze theology. This manuscript copy is in the Robert Garrett collection deposited in the library of Princeton University.

PLATE II.

الأرض اماما موجود الا مولانا الحاكم جل ذكره كان من
الموحدين [illegible] وكتب في شهر كذا او كذا من سنة كذا [illegible]
وكذا من سنين عبد مولانا جل ذكره ومملوكه حمزة ابن
علي ابن احمد هادي المستجيبين المنتقم من المشركين والمرتدين
بسيف مولانا جل ذكره وشدة سلطانه وحده
كتاب المعروف بالنقض الخفي
وقد رفع الى الحضرة اللاهوتية
توكلت على مولانا البار العلام العلي الأعلى حاكم الحكام
من لا يدخل في الخواطر والاوهام حروف بسم الله الرحمن الرحيم
دعاة عبده الامام كتابي البكر معاشر الموحدين لمولانا سبحانه
وحده المستجيبين لحقايق الجواهر الحقيقية الناظرين من نور
الانوار المتشعشعة المتبرين من العلوم المحال المحتوية [illegible]
[illegible] بالاباليس الغوية العابدين للمعبود اله البرية [illegible]
بداية المنفرد عن مبدعاته والذات هو لاهوته والمبدعات [illegible]

Photostatic reproduction of the first page of Ḥamzah's *al-Naqḍ al-Khafi*, the most important production of the founder of the Druze religion. This manuscript copy is in the Robert Garrett collection deposited in the library of Princeton University.

FOREWORD

FOR some nine hundred years, a strange national-religious body has lived in Syria. The Druzes have been the wonder of scholars, and the political opponents of those to whom the country in which they lived belonged. All sorts of theories have been advanced by scholars to account for their peculiar tenets and customs. All sorts of means have been tried by their overlords to put them down. The scholars have been as unsuccessful as have been the overlords; and the Druzes still remain the great mystery of the Lebanon Mountains.

In the following study, a more serious attempt is made to solve the riddle of whom the Druzes are, why they are, and where they are. Professor Hitti is probably better fitted to make this attempt than is any other scholar. Born in the Lebanon Mountains, Arabic is his native tongue. As a boy, and as a young man, he associated with the Druzes. He has had, and still has, access to their literature. It is likely that he knows more about them than they do about themselves. For this reason, I commend the following pages very highly to the attention of all who are concerned about Syria, and who are interested in the history of religion.

RICHARD GOTTHEIL

PREFACE

THIS study is based on two papers: one presented in the annual meeting of the American Historical Association, held at Rochester, New York, December 30, 1926; and the other in the annual meeting of the American Oriental Society, held at Cincinnati, Ohio, April 20, 1927. The thanks of the author are due to Professor Dana C. Munro, President of the American Historical Association; to Professor James A. Montgomery, President of the American Oriental Society; and to Professor Harold H. Bender, Chairman of the Department of Oriental Languages and Literatures at Princeton University, for many valuable suggestions and criticisms. He also wishes to acknowledge with thanks the assistance he received from his wife in verifying references, reading the proofs, and sketching the map inserted in this book.

PRINCETON, May, 1928.

P. K. H.

TABLE OF CONTENTS

Page

Two Facsimile Pages from Druze Manuscripts
Foreword (by Editor of the Studies) III
Preface (by Author) V

CHAPTER I

A UNIQUE AND SECRET SECT

Two Historical Fossils—Relation to World Events—Minor Episodes—Other Secret Sects—Special Interest of this Study 1–4

CHAPTER II

SOCIAL AND HISTORICAL DEVELOPMENT

Feudal Organization—Part Played during the Crusades—The Druze Power at its Height—Banu-Shihāb, the Last Feudal Chiefs—Druzes and Christians Grouped in Political Rather than Religious Parties—The Civil War of 1860 5–9

CHAPTER III

RACIAL ORIGINS

Number and Distribution—Religious and Racial Boundaries Coterminous—Silence of Historians—Travelers' and Scholars' Accounts—Criticism of the Arabian Theory—Diverse Hypotheses—Supposed Relationship with the French and British and with Freemasonry—Other Theories 10–17

CHAPTER IV

THE PERSIAN ORIGIN OF THE DRUZES

The Persian Nucleus at Wādi-al-Taym—The Founders of Druzism All Persian—The Testimony of Religious Vocabulary—Names of Feudal Families—Persian Tribes Transplanted into Syria 18–23

CHAPTER V

DRUZE THEOLOGY AND ITS SOURCES

I. THE PROBLEM WITH ITS DIFFICULTIES

Various Hypotheses—Period of Concealment—Manuscripts—The Historical Setting 24–26

II. THE ḤĀKIM-GOD

Whimsical Character of al-Ḥākim—His Deification—Al-Ḥākim as the Messiah—A Series of Divine Incarnations—The Disappearance and Triumphal Return of al-Ḥākim—Indo-Iranian Influences—Unitarians 26–34

III. FIVE DIVINE MINISTERS AND THREE INFERIOR ONES

The Process of Emanation—The Neo-Platonic Source—Inferior Ministers 34–37

Page

IV. THE PROPHETIC SUCCESSION
Seven Major Prophets—Seven a Sacred Number—Excellence of Druze System—Adam—Jesus 37–39

V. THE INNER MEANING
The Bāṭiniyyah—The Muḥammadan Law Abrogated—The Mystic Element—Sheikhs 40–43

CHAPTER VI
DOGMAS AND PRECEPTS

I. TRANSMIGRATION OF SOULS
Method of Operation—Earlier Moslem Sects Believing in Transmigration—Relation to China 44–47

II. PREDESTINATION AND DISSIMULATION
Shi'ite Contribution 47–48

III. THE CULT OF THE CALF
The Fact—Its Interpretation 49

IV. SEVEN PRECEPTS OF ḤAMZAH
Eight Dogmas—Ḥamzah's Precepts—Sources and Operation 50–51

CHAPTER VII
FOLKLORE

Animism and Saint Worship—Charges of Licentious Practices—Ḥamzites *versus* Darazites—Family Organization—Summary and Conclusion 52–54

APPENDICES
CONTAINING EXTRACTS FROM
THE DRUZE SACRED WRITINGS

APPENDIX A—COVENANT OF INDUCTION INTO THE RELIGION OF THE RULER OF THE AGE 57

APPENDIX B—AL-ḤĀKIM'S ORDINANCE PROHIBITING THE USE OF WINE . 59

APPENDIX C—EXCERPT FROM THE CHARTER FOUND POSTED ON THE WALLS OF THE MOSQUES ON THE OCCASION OF THE DISAPPEARANCE OF OUR LORD AL-IMĀM AL-ḤĀKIM . . . 61

APPENDIX D—EXCERPT FROM THE EPISTLE ENTITLED AL-QUSṬANṬĪNIYYAH ADDRESSED BY BAHĀ'-AL-DĪN TO THE BYZANTINE EMPEROR CONSTANTINE 64

APPENDIX E—EXCERPT FROM BAHĀ'-AL-DĪN'S EPISTLE ENTITLED CHRISTIANITY 68

APPENDIX F—EXHORTATIONS AND PRAYERS BY AL-SAYYID 'ABDULLĀH AL-TANŪKHI 71

Index 75
Map

CHAPTER I

A UNIQUE AND SECRET SECT

Two Historical Fossils:—The Druzes of Syria and the Samaritans of Palestine are two unique communities not to be found elsewhere in the whole world. Like social fossils in an alien environment, these two peoples have survived for hundreds of years in that land rightly described as a "Babel of tongues" and a "museum of nationalities."

The Samaritans are the remnants of the tribes from Assyria and Persia who were transplanted by Sargon some seven hundred years before Christ to take the place of the "ten tribes" who were carried into captivity.[1] They figured in the life of Christ as is illustrated by the case of the "Samaritan woman" and the story of the "good Samaritan." Today they are represented by about one hundred and eighty persons who intermarry among themselves and are becoming rapidly extinct. Their habitat is modern Nāblus (biblical Shechem), and their religion is ancient Judaism mixed with pagan survivals.

The Druzes have no such clear record to show regarding their origin as a people and as a sect. Their ethnographical origins, no less than their ritual practices and religious beliefs, are shrouded in mystery. Appearing for the first time on the pages of history at Wādi-al-Taym near Mt. Hermon in anti-Lebanon, as professors of the divinity of the sixth Fāṭimite Caliph in Cairo (996–1020 A.D.), the Druzes have lived their semi-independent lives secluded in their mountain fastnesses of Lebanon, unmindful of the progress of the world around them, and almost entirely forgotten by the outside world.

---

[1] *Cf.* James A. Montgomery, *The Samaritans, the Earliest Jewish Sect* (Philadelphia, 1907), pp. 46–57.

Hitti.

Relation to World Events:—The few occasions throughout their history in which the Druzes attracted international attention were first at the time of the Crusades, when they were entrusted by the Moslems with the military task of guarding the maritime plain against the Franks. They then fought under the banner of Islam and took part in the attacks against the garrisons of Belfort (*Qal'at al-Shaqīf*) and of Montfort (*Qal'at Qurayn*) in Galilee. Secondly, in the early seventeenth century when their great leader, Fakhr-al-Dīn II (1585–1635), under whom the Druze power reached its zenith, appeared as a refugee from the Sultan of Turkey in the court of the Medicis at Florence. Thirdly, when as a result of their civil wars in 1860 with their Christian neighbors to the north—the Maronites—the French landed a contingent of troops to quell the disturbance which resulted in giving the Lebanon a complete autonomy recognized by the great Powers of Europe. And fourthly, in connection with the recent armed uprising against the French mandate in Syria.

Minor Episodes:—In the local history of Syria and the Lebanon, the Druzes have always figured as a compact and warlike community contriving to enjoy in the fastnesses of their mountain a comparative degree of security and independence. The Latin Kingdom of the Crusades, which with its extensive fiefs formed an elongated strip of land based on the sea and widening on the north to Edessa and on the south to Moab, narrowed in the vicinity of Mt. Hermon, the home of the Druzes. Throughout the Ottoman period (1516–1918) the Druzes and their fellow mountaineers, the Maronites, constituted a thorn in the side of the Turks. The Lebanon enjoyed most of the time local autonomy. Even the Druzes of Ḥawrān, the Bashan of the Bible, were not subject to conscription, and repeatedly refused to pay taxes to the Sublime Porte. When Napoleon in 1798–1799 invaded Egypt and Syria, he sought the aid of the governor of the Lebanon, al-Amīr Bashīr. The Druze resistance to the invasion of the Egyptian army under Ibrāhīm Pasha (1831–1838) was one of the factors in hastening the withdrawal of that army from Syrian soil.

Other Secret Sects:—The Druze people constitute one of the two leading secret sects found only in Syria, the other being the Nuṣayriyyah inhabiting the mountains north of Tripoli. The Ismā'īliyyah of the Ḥimṣ and Ḥamāh district, another secret sect, are descended from the Assassins,[1] who for two centuries or so struck awe and terror into the hearts of the Crusaders, and are represented today by a few other sectarians in Persia and India. The Yezīdis, so-called devil worshipers, practice their hidden rites in the out-of-the-way hills between Antioch and Aleppo and have coreligionists in Kurdistān and Armenia.

Special Interest of this Study:—But of all these sects Druzism is perhaps the most interesting and important. It is still a living force. Its followers form to the present day a vigorous and flourishing community in the Lebanon. Its learned system has not changed since it was first inaugurated in the early part of the eleventh century. The Islam of the Near East has changed and adapted itself to the requirements of the varying conditions. The Christianity of the Near East has changed. But the Druze system has been and still is the same.

The modernizing influence has in late years brought within its sphere quite a large number of the young and uninitiated Druzes. The report of the American University of Beirūt for last year indicates that there are in that institution alone thirty-six Druze students and five Druze teachers. But no one with first-hand knowledge of the situation would go so far as even to recognize the existence of a " modernist movement " alleged to be aiming at divulging the Druze beliefs, much less to declare " It is understood that Dr. Bliss of Beirūt will be the probable intermediary of communication with the western world if this disclosure takes place."[2]

In fact the outside world knows so little about the contents of this religion that in a recent session of the Permanent Mandates

---

[1] Arabic *Ḥashshāshīn* = those addicted to the use of a stupefying weed.

[2] De Lacy O'Leary, *A Short History of the Fatimid Khalifate* (London, 1923), p. 244. Dr. Bliss died in 1920.

Commission of the League of Nations the question was raised as to whether there was anything in the Druze teachings that was inimical to organized government and to state authority.

A study of Druzism is especially valuable and interesting not only because its adherents, unlike the adherents of the other sects, have shown remarkable vitality and thrust themselves repeatedly upon the attention of the world—as in the case of the current events in Syria—but because of its historic connection with Christianity and Oriental Christian sects. In its rise and development from Moslem soil, Druzism held close relationship to Christianity and became heir to a number of Zoroastrian and Judaeo-Christian sects, as well as to a body of Hellenistic and Persian philosophies. Many of those sects and schools of thought have since disappeared, but Druzism is still with us; and, through its medium, their ideas have survived to the present day. The religious and philosophical concepts of many Shī'ite Moslem, and a few semi-Christian, sects have been preserved to us through Druzism, though the original sects and their votaries have long become extinct.

As we shall, therefore, in the following pages analyze and investigate the apparently strange dogmas and tenets of Druze belief, we shall find in addition to Neo-Platonic and Manichaean influences, marked traces of Jewish and Christian influences which have trickled thereto through Moslem strata. The basic fundamentals of Druze theology, as we shall see, are paralleled by corresponding Christian dogmas. One of the founders of Druzism was a renegade Christian, and many of its early leading converts were tribes belonging to some one of the Oriental churches.

There is, after all, nothing mysterious in the " Asian mystery," and the " great enigma " does lend itself to solution.

CHAPTER II

SOCIAL AND HISTORICAL DEVELOPMENT

Feudal Organization:—When we catch our first clear glimpse of the Druze people we find them living—as they are still living today—in small village communities at Wādi-al-Taym and southern Lebanon, organized into a feudal state of society. These village communities were under the control of local sheikhs, themselves subordinate to one or more *amīrs* (princes), and the whole system bound together under a singular form of theocracy. This is still a distinguishing feature of Druze national life.

The early Druze communities flourished at the foot of Mt. Hermon, and in the southern part of Western Lebanon overlooking Beirūt and Sidon. They were in every case agricultural, and subsisted wholly on the produce of the land. Commerce and industry had no attraction to them. These same conditions prevail almost unchanged among the Druzes until the present day. In the lists of the leading merchants of Aleppo, Damascus, Beirūt and Sidon, one would search in vain for a Druze name. Perhaps the greatest merchants that the Druze nation ever produced are Druze immigrants in the United States.

Part Played during the Crusades:—In the early period of the Crusading era, the Druze feudal power was in the hands of two families: the Tanūkhs and the Arislāns. From their fortresses in the Gharb district[1] of southern Lebanon, the Tanūkhs led their incursions into the Phoenician coast and finally succeeded in holding Beirūt and the maritime plain against the Franks.

After the middle of the twelfth century, the Ma'n family superseded the Tanūkhs in Druze leadership. The origin of the

---

[1] The district lying to the west of Beirūt. The ruins of one of these fortresses still crown a little hill near Sarahmūl.

family goes back to a prince Ma'n who made his appearance in the Lebanon in the days of the 'Abbāsid Caliph al-Mustarshid (1118–1135 A.D.), and died in 1149 in the days of Sultan Nūr-al-Dīn of Damascus. The Ma'ns chose for their abode the Shūf district in the southern part of Western Lebanon, overlooking the maritime plain between Beirūt and Sidon, and made their headquarters in Ba'aqlīn, which is still to the present day the leading Druze village. They were invested with feudal jurisdiction by Sultan Nūr-al-Dīn and furnished respectable contingents to the Moslem ranks in their struggle against the Crusaders.

Having cleared Syria from the Franks, the Mamlūk Sultans of Egypt turned their attention to the schismatic Moslems of Syria; and in the year 1305, al-Malik al-Nāṣir inflicted a disastrous defeat on the Druzes at Kasrawān[1] and forced outward compliance on their part to orthodox (Sunni) Islam. Later under the Ottoman Turks they were again chastised severely at 'Ayn-Ṣawfar, in 1585, for having attacked and robbed near Tripoli a body of Janizaries on their way to Constantinople carrying to the imperial treasury taxes collected from Egypt and Syria.

The Druze Power at its Height:—With the advent of the Ottoman Turks and the conquest of Syria by Sultan Selīm I, in 1516, the Ma'ns threw in their lot with the conquering invaders and were immediately acknowledged by the new suzerain as the feudal lords of southern Lebanon. Druze villages spread and prospered in that region, which under Ma'n leadership so flourished that it acquired the generic appellation of Jabal Bayt-Ma'n (the mountain of the Ma'n family) or Jabal al-Durūz. The latter title, however, has since been usurped by the Ḥawrān region which, since the middle of the nineteenth century, has proven a haven of refuge to Druze emigrants from Lebanon and has become the headquarters of Druze power.

Under Fakhr-al-Dīn ibn-Ma'n II (1585–1635) the Druze dominion increased until it included almost all Syria extending from the edge of the Antioch plain in the north to Ṣafad in the south

[1] This region is today entirely occupied by Christians.

with a part of the Syrian desert dominated by Fakhr-al-Dīn's castle at Tadmur (Palmyra), the ancient capital of Zenobia. The ruins of this castle still stand on a steep hill overlooking the town and greet the eye of the passer-by.

Fakhr-al-Dīn became too strong for his Turkish sovereign in Constantinople. He went so far in 1608 as to sign a commercial treaty with Duke Ferdinand I of Tuscany containing secret military clauses. The Sultan then sent a force against him, and he was compelled, in 1614, to flee the land and seek refuge in the courts of Tuscany and Naples.[1]

Fakhr-al-Dīn was the first ruler in modern Lebanon to open the doors of his country to foreign Western influences. Under his auspices the French established a *khān* (hostel) in Sidon, the Florentines a consulate, and the Christian missionaries were admitted into the country. Beirūt and Sidon, which Fakhr-al-Dīn beautified, still bear traces of his benign rule.

Banu-Shihāb, the Last Feudal Chiefs:—As early as the days of Saladin, and while the Ma'ns were still in complete control over southern Lebanon, the Shihāb tribe, originally Ḥijāz Arabs but later domiciled in Ḥawrān, advanced from Ḥawrān, in 1172, and settled in Wādi-al-Taym at the foot of Mt. Hermon. They soon made an alliance with the Ma'ns and were acknowledged the Druze chiefs in Wādi-al-Taym. At the end of the seventeenth century (1697), the Shihābs succeeded the Ma'ns in the feudal leadership of Druze southern Lebanon, though, unlike them, they professed Sunni Islam. Secretly, they showed sympathy with Druzism, the religion of the majority of their subjects. Because of their blood relationship to the Quraysh, the family of the Prophet Muḥammad, the Shihāb, next to the Quraysh, is the noblest family in the Arabic world.

The Shihāb leadership continued till the middle of the last century and culminated in the illustrious governorship of al-Amīr Bashīr (1788–1840) who, after Fakhr-al-Dīn, was the greatest

---

[1] For a biography of Fakhr-al-Dīn, see H. F. Wuestenfeld, *Fachreddin, der Drusenfürst, und seine Zeitgenossen* (Göttingen, 1866).

feudal lord Lebanon produced. Though governor of the Druze mountain, Bashīr was a crypto-Christian, and it was he whose aid Napoleon solicited in 1799 during his campaign against Syria.

Having consolidated his conquests in Syria (1831–1838), Ibrāhīm Pasha, son of the viceroy of Egypt, Muḥammad 'Ali Pasha, made the fatal mistake of trying to disarm the Christians and Druzes of the Lebanon and to draft the latter into his army. This was contrary to the principles of the life of independence which these mountaineers had always lived, and resulted in a general uprising against the Egyptian rule. The uprising was encouraged, for political reasons, by the British. The Druzes of Wādi-al-Taym and Ḥawrān, under the leadership of Shibli al-'Aryān, distinguished themselves in their stubborn resistance at their inaccessible headquarters, al-Laja, lying southeast of Damascus. It is in this same place that the Druzes have for the last two years held out, against the French, under Sulṭān Pasha al-Aṭrash.

Druzes and Christians Grouped in Political Rather than Religious Parties:—The conquest of Syria by the Moslem Arabs in the middle of the seventh century introduced into the land two political factions later called the Qaysites and the Yemenites. The Qaysite party represented the Ḥijāz and Bedouin Arabs who were regarded as inferior by the Yemenites who were earlier and more cultured emigrants into Syria from southern Arabia. The party lines in the Lebanon obliterated racial and religious lines and the people grouped themselves regardless of their religious affiliations, into one or the other of these two parties. The sanguinary feuds between these two factions depleted, in course of time, the manhood of the Lebanon and ended in the decisive battle of 'Ayn-Dārah, in 1711, which resulted in the utter defeat of the Yemenite party. Many Yemenite Druzes thereupon emigrated to the Ḥawrān region and thus laid the foundation of Druze power there.

The Civil War of 1860:—The Druzes and their Christian Maronite neighbors, who had thus far lived as religious communities on amicable terms, entered a period of social disturbance in the year 1840 which culminated in the civil war of 1860. For this disturbance the Sublime Porte in Constantinople was, in a great measure, responsible. The Sultan, realizing that the only way to bring the semi-independent people of the Lebanon under his direct control was to sow the seeds of discord among the people themselves, inaugurated in the mountain a policy long tried and found successful in the Ottoman provinces—the policy of "divide and rule." The civil war of 1860 cost the Christians some ten thousand lives in Damascus, Zaḥlah, Dayr-al-Qamar, Ḥāṣbayya and other towns of the Lebanon. The European powers then determined to interfere and authorized the landing in Beirūt of a body of French troops under General Beaufort d'Hautpoul whose inscription can still be seen on the historic rock at the mouth of the Dog River. Following the recommendations of the powers, the Porte granted Lebanon a local autonomy, guaranteed by the powers, under a Christian governor. This autonomy was maintained until the Great War.

Besides Wādi-al-Taym, the southern part of Western Lebanon and Ḥawrān, the Druzes today occupy a few villages in al-Jabal al-A'la,[1] Mt. Carmel in Palestine, and Ṣafad. Their districts in southern Lebanon are al-Matn and al-Shūf, and their leading villages are: 'Ālayh, Bayṣūr, al-Shuwayfāt, 'Abayh, Ba'aqlīn, and al-Mukhtārah. They number in all Syria and Palestine about 117,000.

---

[1] In the vicinity of Aleppo.

CHAPTER III

RACIAL ORIGINS

Number and Distribution:—With the present numerical strength of the Druzes, their geographical distribution in southern Lebanon, Wādi-al-Taym, al-Jabal al-A'la (between Aleppo and Antioch), Ṣafad and Mt. Carmel in Palestine, and with their later migrations which determined their present habitat, we are more or less familiar. According to the last census there are about 110,000 Druzes in Lebanon and Syria, and 7,000 in Palestine. The present Druze population of Ḥawrān (44,344) are, according to well authenticated documents and local oral tradition,[1] the descendants of emigrants from south Lebanon who, in 1711, as a result of the defeat of their Yemenite party by its Qaysite enemy, left their home, Kafra,[2] and sought a new abode. The number was later augmented by fresh recruits[3] as a result of the 1860 civil war in the Lebanon. Earlier the Jabal al-A'la Druzes emigrated thither from the south.[4] Those of Palestine are of undoubted Lebanese origin, though some of them may have come directly from the Aleppo region.[5] Lebanon therefore was the distributing center of the Druze people and Wādi-al-Taym was the birthplace of their religion.

---

1 Sulaymān abu-'Izz-al-Dīn, "Tawaṭṭun al-Durūz," *al-Kulliyyah* (Beirūt), May, 1926.

2 The ruins of this little village can still be seen near 'Aynāb overlooking Beirūt.

3 Richard F. Burton and Charles F. T. Drake, *Unexplored Syria* (London, 1872), vol. I, 178.

4 *Cf.* Henri Guys, *La Nation Druze, son histoire, sa religion, ses mœurs, et son état politique* (Paris, 1863), p. 25; Gertrude L. Bell, *Syria, the Desert and the Sown* (New York, 1907), p. 306.

5 *Palestine Exploration Fund Quarterly Statement* (London, 1889), p. 123.

It is also easy to trace the ancestry of the modern Druze emigrants in Europe and America back to Syria and the Lebanon. In the United States there are about a thousand Druzes, mostly of Lebanese origin, among whom eighty are women.

The few Druze manuscripts which have thus far fallen into our hands represent the Fāṭimite Ḥākim cult as having spread into many lands outside the confines of Syria, and as having found proselytes throughout northern Africa, Egypt, Arabia, 'Irāq, Persia and other parts of the Near East, into which Ḥamzah had sent missionaries of different grades. That this was not an altogether idle boast is illustrated by a reference in al-Dhahabi[1] († 1345 A.D.) to the execution of all those in far-away Khurāsān who believed in the divinity of al-Ḥākim. Following the example, legendary or historical, of the Prophet Muḥammad, al-Muqtana Bahā'-al-Dīn, the right hand of Ḥamzah in the propagation of the cult, addressed epistles eastward as far as India and westward as far as Constantinople, including one to Constantine VIII[2] and one to Emperor Michael the Paphlagonian.[3] But the fact remains that of those Ḥākim followers, none has survived except the Druzes of the Lebanon.[4] In Egypt they were exterminated soon after the appearance of the cult. No matter where the modern Druze, therefore, may be today, he can rightly trace his origin back to that mountain land of Lebanon.

Religious and Racial Boundaries Coterminous:—This is especially true in view of the fact that with the death of Bahā'-al-Dīn in 1031 A.D. "the door of the Unitarian religion was closed"

---

[1] *Duwal al-Islām* (Ḥayderābād, 1337 A.H.), vol. I, 189.

[2] "L'Épître à Constantin, traité religieux Druze," publié et annoté par les PP. J. Khalīl and L. Ronzevalle, *Mélanges de la Faculté Orientale* (Beirūt, 1909). See *infra*, Appendix D.

[3] The epistles addressed to "the Arabs," "al-Yemen," "India," &c., are all found in "Part I" (*al-Juz' al-Awwal*, MS.) of the seven parts which constitute the collection of tracts and epistles by Bahā'-al-Dīn.

[4] Amīn Bey Kisbāny, a graduate of the American University of Beirūt and former Secretary of King Feiṣal, tells me that he found in the year 1905 in the mountains east of Miknās, Morocco, a Berber tribe, the banu-'Īsa, which claim religious affiliation with the Druzes of Syria.

and no one could be admitted into the Druze fold or permitted exit from it. The Druze religion then ceased to be simply a religion and its followers became a distinct nation.

Bahā'-al-Dīn resorted to this policy as a measure of safety. New pretended converts might betray the cause into the hands of its persecutors. He considered " the day of grace," offered to an unworthy world by the divine al-Ḥākim and the transcendent Ḥamzah, as having passed forever. To a religious body thus reduced to the defensive and desperately striving to conceal its identity, if not its very existence, further proselytism became clearly impossible. The Druze religion thus became wholly hereditary, a sacred privilege, a priceless treasure to be jealously and zealously guarded against the profane. This self-centralization which makes its votaries shun all attempts at increasing their number, coupled with the inviolable secrecy with which they practice their religion, and the readiness with which they ever hold themselves to profess any dominant religion that happens to throw its shadow across their way, has enabled the Druze community to maintain a stable and homogeneous existence for upward of nine centuries. In this it may have had no parallel in the religious history of the world.

Silence of Historians:—The first historian to mention the rise and spread of the Druze religion was Yaḥya ibn-Sa'īd al-Anṭāki,[1] a Christian contemporary of Darazi,[2] the founder of the religion. In his account he was followed by another Christian historian, Jurjus al-Makīn[3] († 1273 A.D.). But both historians are silent on

---

1 " *Ta'rīkh* " in *Corpus Scriptorum Christ. Orient. Scriptores Arabicii Textus*, T. VII (Beirūt, 1909), pp. 180–234.

2 He is the man who gave his name to the sect. Arabic *Durūz* is the plural of *Durzi*.

3 *Ta'rīkh al-Muslimīn* with Latin translation, ed. Erpenius (Leyden, 1625), p. 264. Because of the omission of one dot from the Arabic name of " *Darazi* " in this edition, its pronunciation became " *Darari* " and that is probably why the name occurs in that form in the monumental *Modern Part of the Universal History from the Earliest Account of Time* (65 vols., London, 1747–1768), XIV, 253 and 255 and in the later edition (1779–1884), III, 468, XI, 320. The Druzes are referred to throughout this work as " Dararians."

the question of racial origins. Other Arabic sources, written by Moslems, such as ibn-al-Athīr[1] († 1234), abu-al-Fida[2] († 1331), ibn-Taghri-Birdi[3] († 1469) and later Syrian and Egyptian chroniclers like ibn-Khaldūn († 1406), al-Suyūṭi († 1505), al-Isḥāqi († cir. 1650) are equally silent. To these annalists, questions of religious, and not racial, grouping were the ones of paramount and all-absorbing interest.

The Crusading historians of the West and the reports of the pilgrims likewise throw no light on the subject. To them all non-Christian peoples of Syria were included under the generic name "*Sarraceni.*" The pilgrims ordinarily took the coastal route and were therefore not likely to come much in contact with the Druzes. But the Druzes undoubtedly took part in the struggle against the Crusaders and possibly influenced the Templars by their organization and teaching.[4]

Travelers' and Scholars' Accounts:—Travelers and modern writers have almost exhausted all the list of possible theories in their attempt to explain the racial beginnings of the Druze people. Some have even resorted to fantastic and naïve, if not ludicrous, hypotheses.

Benjamin of Tudela, the Jewish traveler who passed through the Lebanon in or about 1165 was one of the first European writers to refer to the Druzes by name. The word Druzes, in an early Hebrew edition of his travels, occurs as "*Dogziyin,*"[5] but it is clear that this is a scribal error. According to the *Ency-*

---

[1] *Al-Kāmil,* ed. C. J. Tornberg (Leyden, 1863), pp. 81 *seq.*, 147 *seq.*

[2] *Ta'rīkh* (Constantinople, 1286 A.H.), II, 138, 158.

[3] *Al-Nujūm al-Zāhirah,* ed. Popper (Berkeley, the University Press, 1909–1912), II, 69.

[4] C. R. Conder, *The Latin Kingdom of Jerusalem 1099–1291* (London, 1897), pp. 236 and 233.

[5] *The Itinerary of Rabbi Benjamin of Tudela,* translated and edited by A. Asher (London, 1840), I, 29 of Hebrew Text, quoted by J. G. C. Adler, *Monumentum Cuficum Drusorum in Museum Cuficum Borgianum* (Rome, 1782), p. 107. *Cf. The Itinerary of Benjamin of Tudela,* Critical Text, Translation and Commentary, by M. N. Adler (London, 1907), paragraph 29.

clopaedia of Islam,[1] Benjamin also states that the Druzes were descended from the Ituraeans (an Aramean or Arabian tribe which Pompey found in Lebanon in 64 B.C.), but I have not been able to find this statement in any version of Benjamin's *Itinerary*.

Criticism of the Arabian Theory:—Modern travelers like Niebuhr,[2] and scholars like von Oppenheim,[3] undoubtedly echoing the popular Druze belief regarding their own origin, have classified them as Arabs. The prevailing idea among the Druzes themselves today is that they are of Arab stock. This hypothesis conforms to the general local tradition, but is in contradiction to the results obtained in this study. In his Huxley Memorial Lecture, "The Early Inhabitants of Western Asia," Professor Felix von Luschan, the famous anthropologist of the University of Berlin, states that he measured the skulls of fifty-nine adult male Druzes and "not one single man fell, as regards his cephalic index, within the range of the real Arab."[4] Evidently the Druze claim of Arab descent is the result of their application of the principle of dissimulation (*taqiyyah*) to their racial problem, they being a small minority amidst an Arab majority which has always been in the ascendancy. According to this principle, one is not only ethically justified but is under obligation, when the exigencies of the case require, to conceal the reality of his religion, or race, and feign other religious or racial relationships.

The writer remembers hearing Druzes in Lebanon discussing Japanese victories during the Russo-Japanese War of 1906 and claiming common origin with the yellow Far Easterners. Miss Bell who was then traveling in Ḥawrān (Jabal al-Durūz) observed that the "Druzes believe the Japanese to belong to their own race."[5]

---

1 Article "Druzes" by Baron Carra de Vaux.

2 *Travels through Arabia and other Countries in the East*, Trans. by R. Heron (Edinburgh, 1792), II, 179.

3 Max F. von Oppenheim, *Vom Mittelmeer zum Persischen Golf* (Berlin, 1899), I, 111 *seq.*

4 *Journal of the Royal Anthropological Institute* (London, 1911), p. 232.

5 *Syria, the Desert and the Sown*, *op. cit.*, p. 103.

Diverse Hypotheses:—Lamartine[1] discovered in the modern Druzes the remnants of the Samaritans; the Earl of Carnarvon,[2] those of the Cuthites[3] whom Esarhaddon transplanted into Palestine; George Washington Chasseaud,[4] those of the Hivites; and Mrs. Worsley,[5] those of the Hittites. Drawing his conclusions from anthropometric measurements, Professor Luschan makes the Druzes, Maronites, and Nuṣayriyyah of Syria—together with the Armenians, Ṭahtājis, Bektāshis, 'Ali-Ilāhis and Yezīdis of Asia Minor and Persia—" with their enormous high and short heads and narrow and high noses "—the modern representatives of the ancient Hittites.[6] Captain Light describes them on the authority of Pococke " as the remnant of Israel who fled the wrath of Moses after the destruction of the molten calf."[7] Canon Parfit, who lived several years among the Druzes, states in a recent book that they are " the descendants of Arabs, Persians, Hindoos, Jews and Christians."[8]

Supposed Relationship with the French and British and with Freemasonry:—Deceived by superficial and purely accidental phonetic resemblances, certain French scholars once accepted the curious hypothesis, which in the seventeenth century found vogue in Europe, to the effect that the modern Druzes of the Lebanon are the descendants of a Latin colony which owed its origin to a comte de Dreux who, subsequent to the fall of Acre, led his Crusading regiment to the out-of-the-way hills of Lebanon. The

---

[1] *Voyage, op. cit.*, II, 109.

[2] *Recollections of the Druses of Lebanon* (London, 1860), pp. 42–43.

[3] II Kings 17:24.

[4] *The Druzes of Lebanon, their Manners, Customs and Religion with a Translation of their Religious Code* (London, 1855), p. 97.

[5] This lady dragged her husband some fifty years ago from a comfortable home in London and established herself in a Druze village, 'Ayn-'Unūb, a few miles from Beirūt in order to prove her theory. See J. T. Parfit, *Among the Druzes of Lebanon and Bashan* (London, 1917), p. 33.

[6] *Journal Royal Anthropological Institute* (London, 1911), *op. cit.*, p. 241.

[7] Henry Light, *Travels in Egypt, Nubia, Holy Land, Mount Libanon and Cyprus in the Year 1814* (London, 1818), p. 225.

[8] Parfit, *Among the Druzes, op. cit.*, p. 33.

same myth makes the Druze chief Fakhr-al-Dīn a scion of the house of Lorraine through Godfrey of Bouillon.

This genealogy was apparently fabricated in connection with the visit of that prince Fakhr-al-Dīn to Italy, after he had made an alliance in 1608 with Ferdinand I, Grand Duke of Tuscany, with a view to arousing a crusade against Fakhr-al-Dīn's enemy suzerains, the Turks. In 1763 Puget de Saint-Pierre wrote a book entitled *Histoire des Druses, Peuple du Liban, formé par une colonie de François* (Paris). Articles appeared in learned magazines[1] supporting the idea. More discriminating writers like Volney,[2] Lamartine,[3] Dussaud,[4] were quick to detect the historic impossibility of the hypothesis. English travelers like Maundrell[5] and Pococke[6] seem to have accepted the theory of Druze descent from the remains of some Christian army of Crusading origin.

It was evidently in an analogous sphere of ideas that such lodges as those of "*Druzes Réunis*" and "*Commandeurs du Liban*" were founded in France.[7]

By the same processes of reasoning the Druze name was connected with those of the Druids, and many Freemason lodges have claimed relationship with the Druzes whose "ancestors were none other than the original subjects of King Hiram of Tyre, the builders of Solomon's temple."[8]

The writer remembers more than one occasion on which prominent contemporaneous Druzes claimed common descent for their people with the British. That this claim goes back to the

---

1 "Religion des Druses," *Revue de l'Orient* (Paris, 1846), X, 240.

2 *Voyage en Égypte et en Syrie pendant les années 1783, 1784 et 1785* (*Œuvres de C. F. Volney*, deuxième éd., tome II, Paris, 1825), I, 397.

3 Lamartine, *Voyage en Orient 1832–1833, Œuvres Complètes*, tome 7, II, 104.

4 R. Dussaud, *Histoire et Religion des Nosairis* (Paris, 1904), p. 8, n. 2.

5 Henry Maundrell, *A Journey from Aleppo to Jerusalem on Easter A.D. 1697* (London, 1810), pp. 51–52.

6 Richard Pococke, *A Description of the East and Some Other Countries* (London, 1745), p. 94.

7 Vital Cuinet, *Syrie, Liban et Palestine* (Paris, 1890), p. 313.

8 B. H. Springett, *Secret Sects of Syria* (London, 1922), Chap. XXV, "The Relation of the Druzes to Freemasonry."

early part of the eighteenth century is shown by a reference in Pococke's *Description*.[1] English agents in Syria, anxious for a " zone of influence " among the Druzes to counteract the French zone among the Maronites, may have acquiesced in the Druze claim to blood relationship with the British.

Other Theories:—Some English scholars[2] of the eighteenth century tried to relate the Druzes to the *Derusaiaioi* mentioned by Herodotus[3] as one of the Median tribes transplanted by Cyrus. In this as in the preceding cases, there seems to be no justification for the theory beyond the apparent similarity in names.

More worthy of consideration is the statement of Hogarth and Gertrude Bell in the *Encyclopaedia Britannica*[4] that the Druzes are a mixture of stocks in which the Arab largely predominates " grafted on to an original mountain population of Aramaic blood." A study, however, of the Arabic colloquial used by the modern Druzes of Lebanon reveals no such marked Aramaisms as is revealed by a study of the colloquial of their northern neighbors, the Maronites, who are of mixed Aramaic stock; and there is nothing in the sources at our command to justify the inclusion of the Aramaic blood to such an extent in the Druze veins.

---

1 *Op. cit.*, p. 94.
2 Adler, *op. cit.*, p. 106.
3 *Historiae, lib.* I, *cap.* CXXV.
4 (Eleventh edition), article " Druses."

Chapter IV

THE PERSIAN ORIGIN OF THE DRUZES

What then are the racial affinities of that singular people which for the last nine hundred years has grouped itself with marvelous cohesion, solidarity and consciousness of kind, around the divine person of a whimsical Caliph? Or, to reduce our question to its lowest denomination, what were the racial connections of that little community at the foot of Mt. Hermon, in Wādi-al-Taym, which in 407 A.H.[1]/1016 A.D. responded to the mission of Darazi and consequently assumed his name?

The Persian Nucleus at Wādi-al-Taym:—It is safe for us to make two postulates at the very outset. First, the people who later became known as the "Druzes" must have formed a more or less socially homogeneous community prior to the advent of Darazi. Second, that homogeneous community must have had in it something which predisposed it for the favorable reception of the seemingly strange and peculiar doctrines proclaimed by Darazi, and, having accepted them, to cherish and perpetuate those doctrines. Something in the social and intellectual make-up of that primitive community at Wādi-al-Taym must have made it respond whole-heartedly to Druzism and proved a fertile soil for the germination of its dogmas.

The trustworthy Egyptian historian, ibn-Taghri-Birdi († 1469 A.D.), who is the first authority to give us any explanation as to why al-Ḥākim chose, of all places, Wādi-al-Taym as the scene for his Syrian propaganda, gives that explanation, which he, of course, draws from earlier documents, in the following words:

[1] Ḥamzah did not proclaim openly the incarnation of the Deity in al-Ḥākim till the following year, 408 A.H., which marks the beginning of the Druze era and from which their manuscripts are dated.

"And al-Ḥākim said to Darazi, 'Proceed into Syria and spread the cause in the mountains because their people are quick to follow.'"[1] This reason may sound strange considering the rightly reputed conservative character of mountaineers, but at least it makes it clear that Darazi proceeded to Wādi-al-Taym according to preconceived plans and he made its population his first objective. And since his new doctrine was at the core an incarnational one of the extreme Shī'ite type which had been previously developed in 'Irāq and Persia, it is logical to assume that the natives of Wādi-al-Taym must have been subjected to 'Irāqizing or Persianizing influence before.

The Founders of Druzism All Persian:—It should also be remembered in this connection that Darazi himself was of Turco-Persian origin.[2] His sect was the Ismā'īliyyah.[3] His theological philosophy was Bāṭiniyyah (Innerite), *i.e.*, the system of giving an esoteric, inner meaning to the scriptures other than the apparent, literal one. Ḥamzah, the teacher of Darazi[4] and the brains of the whole movement, especially after Darazi had fallen into disrepute, was of undoubted Persian origin.[5] Besides, the whole

---

[1] *Al-Nujūm al-Zāhirah, op. cit.*, II, 69.

[2] Al-Makīn, *op. cit.*, calls him Persian; Silvestre de Sacy, *Exposé de la religion des Druzes* (2 vols., Paris, 1838), I, CCLXXXIV, thinks he was a Turk. By many historians he is described *min muwalladi al-atrāk*, *i.e.*, one of his parents was Turkish, of course, not Ottoman Turkish, but one from Persia or Turkestan. See al-Muḥibbi, *Khulāṣat al-Athar* (Cairo, 1284 A.H.), p. 268.

[3] A Shī'ah sect which believed in seven Imāms of whom the last and greatest was Muḥammad ibn-Ismā'īl, a descendant of 'Ali. For a statement in English on this sect see D. B. Macdonald, *Muslim Theology, Jurisprudence and Constitutional Theory* (New York, 1903), pp. 43 *seq.* and E. G. Browne, *A Literary History of Persia from the Earliest Times until Firdawsi* (New York, 1902), pp. 405–415.

[4] In his *Literary History of Persia from the Earliest Times until Firdawsi, op. cit.*, p. 400, and *Literary History of Persia from Firdawsi to Sa'di* (New York, 1906), p. 199, the eminent English scholar, E. G. Browne, confuses Darazi with Ḥamzah making them both one man "Hamzah-al-Duruzi."

[5] Many historians refer to him as "al-Zūzani," *i.e.*, coming from Zūzan in Persia. *The Governors and Judges of Egypt or Kitāb al-Wulāh wa-Kitāb al-Quḍāh of el-Kindi*, together with an appendix derived mostly from *Raf' El-Iṣr* by Ibn-Ḥajar, ed. R. Guest (Beirūt, 1908), p. 612.

Fāṭimite dynasty, whose claim of legitimacy of descent from 'Ali and Fāṭimah has been either suspected or vehemently denied by many judicious Moslem historians, was probably founded by, and descended from, a Persian adventurous ancestor who exploited a 'Alid tradition and a 'Alid fetish for his own personal interest and for the aggrandizement of his progeny.

The Testimony of Religious Vocabulary:—If we, furthermore, investigate the technical terms current in the Druze religious vocabulary, we find many of them, including the word for God, *al-Bār* (from Barkhoda),[1] of clear Persian origin.[2] It is significant that the Druze password as taught in their catechism, formulated after the time of Ḥamzah and al-Muqtana and patterned after the Christian system of questions and answers, consists in the proper answer to the catch question, "Do they plant the seeds of *halālij* [or *ihlīlij*, from Persian *halīlah* = *myrobalan citrina*] in your country?"[3] If the man is a Druze his answer would be, "Yes, they are planted in the hearts of the believers."

Names of Feudal Families:—A study, therefore, of the Druze dogmas, their religious vocabulary and the nationality of the missionaries would suggest 'Irāqi and Persian beginnings for the Druze people. This conclusion regarding the Persian racial origins of the Druzes which we have reached is in contradiction to almost all other conclusions reached by travelers and historians.[4] It is

---

[1] E. Blochet, *Le Messianisme dans l'hétérodoxie musulmane* (Paris, 1903), p. 94, n. 1; S. de Sacy, *Chrestomathie Arabe* (Paris, 1826), II, 246, n. 72.

[2] This etymology is recognized by Ḥamzah himself in *al-Sīrah al-Mustaqīmah*, MS.

[3] One version of the Druze catechism was translated by Adler, *op. cit.*, see p. 127; another by Guys, *La Nation Druse*, see p. 199. *Cf.* Baron de Bock, *Essai sur l'histoire du Sabéisme auquel on a joint un catéchisme, qui contient les principaux dogmes de la religion des Druzes* (Metz, 1788), pp. 143 *seq.*; "A Catechism of the Druze Religion" in *Palestine Exploration Fund Quarterly Statement* (London, 1886), p. 41.

[4] Lieut.-Col. Conder in his *Latin Kingdom of Jerusalem*, *op. cit.*, p. 235, makes the categorical statement "Nor were the Druzes of Arab race. They were in great measure of Persian stock; and their women wore the silver horn beneath the veil, projecting forward from the forehead, a costume which was used among tribes of the Oxus and Caspian."

further corroborated by an investigation of the genealogies of the chief feudal families which we shall now consider.

The leading families among the Druzes have been throughout their history either of full Kurdish and Persian origin or of Persianized and 'Irāqized Arab origin. That is, they have been either Kurdish and Persian families or tribes from the Arabian peninsula who, before their advent into the Lebanon, sojourned for many generations in Mesopotamia where they became fully indoctrinated with the 'Alid ideas and subjected to Gnostic and Manichaean influences.

Wādi-al-Taym, the place where the Druzes first appear in history under that name,[1] is so called after an Arab tribe Taym-Allāh (formerly Taym-Allāt) which, according to the greatest Arab historian, al-Ṭabari,[2] first came from Arabia into the valley of the Euphrates where they were Christianized prior to their migration into the Lebanon. Many of the Druze feudal families whose genealogies have been preserved to us by the two modern Syrian chroniclers: al-Amīr Ḥaydar and al-Shidyāq, seem also to point in the direction of the same origin—Arabian tribes which emigrated *via* the Persian Gulf and stopped in 'Irāq on the route that was later to lead them to Syria. The first feudal Druze family, the banu-Tanūkh, which made for itself a name in fighting the Crusaders under authorization from the Sultan Nūr-al-Dīn of Damascus, was according to Ḥaydar,[3] an Arab tribe from al-Ḥīrah (Mesopotamia) where it occupied the position of a ruling family and was apparently christianized. The Tanūkhs must have left Arabia as early as the second or third century A.D. The Ma'n tribe which superseded the Tanūkhs and produced the greatest Druze hero in history, Fakhr-al-Dīn, had the same traditional origin,[4] although Fakhr-al-Dīn himself is quoted, on the authority

---

[1] For *Tayāminah* (coming from, or belonging to, Wādi-al-Taym) as a synonym of "Druzes," see al-Muḥibbi, *Khulāṣat al-Athar* (Cairo, 1284 A.H.), III, 268. *Cf.* Guys, *La Nation Druze*, p. 118.

[2] *Ta'rīkh al-Rusul*, ed. de Goeje (Leyden, 1889), I, 2489–2490, 2031.

[3] *Ta'rīkh* (Cairo, 1900), p. 350.

[4] Ḥaydar, p. 316. See also T. Shidyāq, *Akhbār al-A'yān* (Beirūt, 1859), p. 162.

of a grandson of his, as saying that the Ma'ns were Kurds.[1] The banu-Talḥūq[2] and 'Abd-al-Malik[3] who supplied the later Druze leadership have the same record as the Tanūkhs. The banu-'Imād are so-called from al-'Imādiyyah,[4] near al-Mawṣil, and, like the Junblāṭs,[5] are of Kurdish origin. The Arislāns claim descent from the Ḥīrah Arab kings, but the name (*Arslan* = lion) suggests Persian influence if not origin. It was in conformity with the principle of racial dissimulation (*taqiyyah*) that many Druze families of Kurdish and Persian origins claimed Arab descent.

It is interesting to note that most of these Druze Arab tribes trace their origin to southern Arabia, and not to the Ḥijāz tribes which flooded western Asia at the time of the Moslem conquests. This would imply an earlier migration into 'Irāq than the rise of Islam, and a sojourn of many generations in a sphere of Persian influence.

Persian Tribes Transplanted into Syria:—That the Indo-Iranian elements in the blood of the historic Druzes are varied and multiplied can be safely assumed, not only on the ground of probable beginning and intermarriages in their earlier home, Mesopotamia, but on the ground of possible admixture in Syria itself where many Persians had been domiciled prior to the rise of Druzism. Al-Balādhuri, the most judicious of the early Arab historians, informs us that Mu'āwiyah (660–680 A.D.), among other Umayyad Caliphs, transplanted on different occasions quite a number of Persian and Mesopotamian tribes into the districts of Ba'labakk, Ḥimṣ, Ṣūr (Tyre) and elsewhere in order, evidently, to take the place of the Byzantines who had evacuated Syria subsequent to its conquest by the Moslem Arabs.[6] In the shuffle to which these

---

[1] Al-Muḥibbi, *op. cit.*, p. 266.

[2] Shidyāq, p. 155.

[3] Shidyāq, p. 160.

[4] Shidyāq, p. 160.

[5] Baron Carra de Vaux, *Les Penseurs de l'Islam* (Paris, 1926), V, 69, erroneously makes the Junblāṭs Moslem. They and the Arislāns form the two leading Druze families at the present time.

[6] Philip K. Hitti, *Origins of the Islamic State* (New York, 1916), pp. 180, 260. Ya'qūbi, *Kitāb al-Buldān*, ed. Juynboll (Leyden, 1886), pp. 114–115.

Persian tribes were later subjected in Syria,[1] it is possible that some tribes landed in Wādi-al-Taym, which, according to a passage in ibn-al-Athīr,[2] recorded under the events of 523 A.H./1128 A.D., was included in the district of Ba'labakk. According to the same passage, Wādi-al-Taym was then swarming with diverse heterodoxies, such as the "Nuṣayriyyah, Durziyyah and Majūs" (Magians = Manichaeans or some Zoroastrian sect). The modern Shī'ah of Syria, popularly known as "Matāwilah" may go back to one or more of these transplanted Persian tribes.[3]

Racially, therefore, the Druze people were a mixture of Persians, 'Irāqis, and Persianized Arabs, and were thereby admirably fitted for the reception of the Druze dogmas and tenets of belief, which we shall next take up.

---

[1] Hitti, *Origins*, p. 228.

[2] *Al-Kāmil*, ed. Tornberg (Leyden, 1863), X, 461–462.

[3] Père Lammens, *Tasrīḥ al-Abṣār* (Beirūt, 1914), II, 48–49. *Cf.* Lammens, *La Syrie* (Beirūt, 1921), I, 182.

Chapter V

DRUZE THEOLOGY AND ITS SOURCES

I. THE PROBLEM WITH ITS DIFFICULTIES

Various Hypotheses:—As in the case of determining the racial origins of the Druze people, so in the case of ascertaining the origin of their religion, all kinds of theories, some curious and amusing, others fantastic and naïve, have been proposed. By different authors at different times the Druze religion was thought to be related to ancient Judaism, Samaritanism and Mandaeism.[1] Madame Blavatsky, the founder of theosophy, traces, in an early issue of *The Theosophist*, the Druze religion back to Tibetan Lamaism.[2] Others have declared the whole thing an "enigma hardly possible to explain."[3]

Period of Concealment:—The difficulties in the way of reaching a thorough and scientific appreciation of the Druze religion are due to the scarcity of outside sources, to the secrecy with which the Druzes themselves practice their religious rites and mystic ceremonies, to the carefulness with which they guard their sacred writings against the profane, to the allegorical and esoteric character of the Arabic style of the few manuscripts which have fallen into our hands, and to the legitimate practice of *taqiyyah*, or dissimulation (according to which a member of this religion is free to profess publicly any other dogma or creed if therein lies the path of safety)—all these conspire to make the Druze riddle

---

[1] Court de Gebelin in *Monde primitif*, t. 8, p. 3, tries to make it a branch of "Sabéisme." *Cf.* Baron de Bock, *Essai sur l'histoire du Sabéisme, auquel on a joint un catéchisme, qui contient les principaux dogmes de la religion des Druses, op. cit.*, pp. 136 *seq.*

[2] Springett, *Secret Sects of Syria*, pp. 234–247.

[3] Guys, *La Nation Druse*, pp. 13–15.

one of the most baffling in the history of religious thought.[1] According to Druze teaching, they are now, pending the "absence" of al-Ḥākim, in a "period of concealment" (*zamān al-sitr*) and nothing of their religion should be divulged or promulgated.

Manuscripts:—Almost the only sources, therefore, consist of the manuscripts of a hundred or so texts, many of which are didactic and polemic treatises, which as a result of local disturbances in the Druze region, particularly the invasion of Ibrāhīm Pasha, 1831–1838, and the civil war of 1860, found their way into the hands of scholars. One of the first manuscripts to be carried into Europe was presented in 1700 to Louis XIV by a Syrian physician, and is now deposited in the Bibliothèque Nationale. Most of these manuscripts are written in a language which from the standpoint of diction, grammar and style is quite far from the language of the Koran and bristles with contradictory and obscure passages, cryptic phrases, and ambiguous words. The present study is based on twenty or more original manuscripts, many of which are in the Robert Garrett collection at Princeton University.

The Historical Setting:—Viewed as a distinct religious phenomenon, as an independent sphere of thought detached from its historical setting and background, Druzism does present somewhat of an enigma; but considered as an outgrowth of the Ismā'īliyyah sect, which itself belonged to the ultra group of the Shī'ah heterodoxies of Islam, and properly envisaged in the Moslem *milieu* out of which it arose and in which it developed, the Druze religion yields to analytical treatment and becomes comparatively easy of explanation.

Silvestre de Sacy, the father of Arabic scholarship in Europe, whose monumental work *Exposé de la religion des Druzes* (2 vols., Paris, 1838) has not yet been superseded though it appeared some

---

[1] True to the principle of *taqiyyah*, Ṣāliḥ ibn-Yaḥya, himself probably a Druze, from whose pen we have the best history of Beirūt (*Ta'rīkh*, ed. Cheikho, Beirūt, 1902) written in the fifteenth century, does not even mention the Druzes by name.

ninety years ago and before many original sources were brought to light, gives us an excellent internal interpretation of the Druze religion but does not go far in disentangling the different fibers in the intricate and complex web of the system and in tracing them back to the remote origins in the various religions or philosophical and metaphysical schools of thought. And whereas many eminent scholars in recent times, chief among whom stands the late Ignacz Goldziher of the University of Budapest, have addressed themselves to the task of analyzing the component elements that entered into the composition of Sunni (orthodox) and Shi'ite Islam, the Druze sect still remains without an interpreter in the field of the history of religion.

II. THE ḤĀKIM-GOD

Whimsical Character of al-Ḥākim:—The basic and distinctive dogma of Druze theology is the deification of the young Fāṭimite Caliph (996–1020).

Sunni Moslem historians, such as al-Dhahabi, ibn-al-Athīr, abu-al-Fida, ibn-al-Qalānisi,[1] al-Rūdhrāwari[2] and ibn-Khallikān,[3] remembering him as the heretic who abolished the five pillars of Islam and ordered the names of the early Caliphs associated with a curse in the public prayer, have portrayed him in terms of a medieval Nero, tyrannical and unbalanced to the point of mental derangement. The Christian historians, such as Yaḥya ibn-Sa'īd,[4] al-Makīn[5] and Bar-Hebraeus,[6] associating his memory with the destruction of the Holy Sepulchre in Jerusalem "leaving not one stone upon another"[7] and the revival of the old regulations,

---

1 *Dhayl Ta'rīkh Dimashq*, ed. H. F. Amedroz (Beirūt, 1908), pp. 44–50, 55–71.

2 *Dhayl Kitāb Tajārib al-Umam*, ed. Amedroz (Oxford, 1921), III, 233 *seq.*, English translation by D. S. Margoliouth, vol. VI, 246–247.

3 *Wafayāt al-A'yān* (Cairo, 1299 A.H.), III, 4–7, English translation by MacGuckin de Slane (4 vols., Paris, 1842–1871), III, 449 *seq.*

4 *Op. cit.*

5 *Op. cit.*

6 Abu-al-Faraj ibn-al-'Ibri, *Mukhtaṣar al-Duwal* (Beirūt, 1890), pp. 312–313.

7 Al-Qalānisi, *op. cit.*, p. 67.

first enacted by the 'Abbāsid al-Mutawakkil, which made it incumbent upon all Christians to wear distinctively colored clothes with heavy wooden crosses dangling from their necks, were equally merciless in his condemnation. Through Gibbon,[1] who paints quite a dark picture of al-Ḥākim, the English-speaking world has become acquainted with him as a bizarre and whimsical character. What we have from the pen of these writers is not a portrait but a caricature.

The Druze writers, while not denying some of his excesses, interpret them allegorically and symbolically.[2] His freakishness only serves to intensify the belief in his superhuman character. His extraordinary conduct proves his divine nature.

The fact that al-Ḥākim introduced many reforms regulating weights and measures, fought immorality with police ordinances and succeeded in establishing a religious community that has survived for nine centuries like a fossil—and if ever there was a fossil in history that certainly is the Druze community—amidst a hostile environment indicates that he was not the kind of a maniac or fool whose biography these early writers have left us. (See Appendix B.)

His Deification:—Strange as the apotheosis of al-Ḥākim may seem—especially in view of the black picture left us by his biographies—yet the idea itself was not a novel one in Islam. Prior to the rise of Druzism, different Shī'ah sects have held different shades of the belief that 'Ali and his successor *Imāms* were infallible supernatural beings endowed to some degree with the divine essence. The Ismā'īliyyah sect, from whose bosom Druzism sprang as did also the Assassins of Crusading fame, together with al-Qarāmiṭah, which between the ninth and twelfth centuries swept through Western Asia, had both venerated certain descendants of 'Ali and hailed them as infallible rulers of the world.

---

[1] *Decline and Fall of the Roman Empire*, ed. H. H. Milman (a new edition in five volumes, New York, 1845), IV, 173.

[2] Ḥamzah, *Kitāb fīhi Ḥaqā'iq Ma*, MS.

The step from that position to an incarnational philosophy of theism is not, indeed, a long one; and a few of the extremist (*Ghulāt*) Shī'ah sects had taken it. In the polemic literature of Islam, and particularly in the works of al-Baghdādi[1] († 1037 A.D.), ibn-Ḥazm[2] († 1063) and al-Shahrastāni[3] († 1153), we have preserved for us among the semi-religious, semi-philosophical sects of unorthodox Islam the names of many groups with incarnational theories which may be considered the prototypes of the Druze al-Ḥākim cult. First among these was al-Saba'iyyah, so called after a Jew who declared 'Ali god. Al-Baghdādi[4] devotes a chapter to the incarnational sects (*al-Ḥulūliyyah*) and enumerates ten different ones.

The Nuṣayriyyah, who preceded the Druzes and had early contacts with them, as attested by the Druze manuscripts,[5] and who are represented until the present day by three villages[6] in the Druze district at Wādi-al-Taym, deify 'Ali.[7] 'Ali-God adherents are also to be found today in a sect of Turcoman peasants at Qars (Ardaghān) whose very name "'Ali-Ilāhi"[8] betrays their characteristic belief.

Even in other than Shī'ite circles of Islam, the elevation of a mortal to the ranks of the deity finds not an altogether

---

[1] *Mukhtaṣar al-Farq bayn al-Firaq*, ed. Philip K. Hitti (Cairo, 1924). Al-Baghdādi, *al-Farq bayn al-Firaq*, ed. Bedr (Cairo, 1910), partly done into English by Kate Chambers Seelye and entitled *Moslem Schisms and Sects* (New York, 1920).

[2] *Al-Fiṣal fi al-Milal* (Cairo, 1317 A.H.).

[3] *Al-Milal w-al-Niḥal*, on the margin of ibn-Ḥazm. Translated by T. Haarbrücker under the title *Asch-Schahrastāni, Religionspartheien und Philosophen-Schulen* (Halle, 1850).

[4] Ed. Hitti, *op. cit.*, pp. 160–161.

[5] An early Druze MS. *al-Radd 'ala al-Risālah al-Dāmighah li-al-Fāsiq al-Nuṣayri* was written by Ḥamzah to refute the charges of a Nuṣayri.

[6] These are: 'Aynfīt, Za'ūra and Ghajar. They lie not far from Bāniyās, ancient Caesarea Philippi.

[7] R. Dussaud, *Histoire et Religion des Nosairis* (Paris, 1904), p. 53.

[8] Saeed Khan, "The Sect of Ahl-i-Ḥaqq" in *The Moslem World* (New York), Jan., 1927, pp. 31–42.

uncommon expression. The case of the Ṣūfi al-Ḥallāj,[1] who was crucified in Baghdād in 922 A.D. because he identified himself with God, and his fellow self-deified Ṣūfi, al-Shalmaghāni,[2] who was beheaded also in Baghdād in 934 A.D., may be cited as illustrations.

Al-Ḥākim as the Messiah:—Having determined the antecedents of the Druze incarnational dogma in the preceding Islamic thought, our next task is to push back our query into the intellectual ancestry of that Islamic idea in the pre-Islamic realm of thinking. The influence of the Christian incarnation precedent must have been too widespread and too apparent to have escaped the attention of the early Moslem thinkers. The great ibn-Khaldūn and before him al-Shahrastāni[3] blame the incarnational Moslem heresy on Judaeo-Christian sects. Among modern Western scholars, de Sacy,[4] van Vloten[5] and Goldziher[6] have laid great stress on the Messianic tendencies in early Islam as the main source of Shī'ism. In the case of the Druzes, Ḥamzah, of course with an eye upon the Copts of Egypt and other Christians, goes so far as to declare al-Ḥākim "the Messiah."[7]

His argument in defense of deification is clever:—"If ye Christians and Jews believe that God spoke to Moses through a dry tree and, on another occasion, through a mountain..., is it not then meet to believe that our Lord [al-Ḥākim] is a more worthy means through whom God manifests to the world his power and behind whom he conceals himself?"[8]

---

[1] Abu-al-Fida, *op. cit.*, II, 75; ibn-Khallikān, *op. cit.*, I, 261 *seq.* = de Slane Translation, I, 423 *seq.*; De Lacy O'Leary, *Arab Thought and its Place in History* (London, 1922), p. 193; L. Massignon, *al-Ḥallāj* (Paris, 1922), vol. I, pp. 292–329.

[2] Yāqūt, *Mu'jam al-Udabā*, ed. Margoliouth (Leyden, 1907), I, 302; Duncan B. Macdonald, *op. cit.*, p. 185.

[3] *Op. cit.*, II, 10.

[4] *Exposé*, I, XXXI *seq.*

[5] *Recherches sur la domination arabe, le chiitisme et les croyances messianiques sous le khalifat des omayyades* (Amsterdam, 1894), pp. 54 *seq.*

[6] *Vorlesungen über den Islam* (2nd ed., Heidelberg, 1925), pp. 3, 17, 120 and Chap. V, "Das Sektenwesen."

[7] Ḥamzah, *Khabar al-Yahūd w-al-Naṣāra*, MS.

[8] *Kashf al-Haqā'iq* in C. Seybold, "Die Drusenschrift," *Kitāb al-Noqaṭ* (Leipzig, 1902), p. 92.

In the Druze catechism, al-Ḥākim is repeatedly identified with "the living Messiah."[1] Likewise Bahā'-al-Dīn, in his turn, identifies Ḥamzah with the Messiah.[2] In his many epistles directed to the Christians, Bahā'-al-Dīn often calls the Christians "saints" and "assemblies of saints." (See Appendix D.)

A Series of Divine Incarnations:—The guiding thought of Druze theogony, as it was with the Ismā'īliyyah, is the belief in a succession of divine manifestations through a progressive series. Hence with the Druzes, al-Ḥākim is not only the incarnation of God but the final and most perfect manifestation, having been preceded by nine others among whom figure al-Bār (Barkhoda), 'Ali and the ancestors of al-Ḥākim in the Fāṭimite Caliphate.

According to a further development of this idea, the divine humanity of God, though it appears under different names in different countries and times, is essentially one and always the same in its diverse manifestations. The human figure serves only as a veil to hide the divine essence behind.

In contrast to the Druze ten successive incarnations, the Nuṣayriyyah believe in seven only, corresponding to the seven heavens and the seven planets.[3]

To this same sphere of thought should be consigned the recent Bahā'i theory of divine manifestations which is an outgrowth of Bābi and Sheikhite ideas which in turn flourished in the fertile Shī'ah soil of Persia. And as in modern Bahā'ism so in ancient Druzism, resort is had to Pythagorean subtleties and to the occult art of manipulating letters and combinations of letters assigning cabalistic numerical values[4] to them in order to

---

[1] Adler, *op. cit.*, pp. 121, 132.

[2] See his epistle entitled *al-Masīḥiyyah* (Christianity), MS., and Appendix E.

[3] Dr. Wolff, "Auszüge aus dem Katechismus der Nossairier," *Zeitschrift der Deutschen morgenländischen Gesellschaft* (1849), III, 303.

[4] This science is represented in Islam by the "Ḥurūfi" school and the Bektāshi order of dervishes. See Goldziher, *Vorlesungen*, pp. 246, 274, 362; E. G. Browne, *Persian Literature under Tartar Dominion* (Cambridge University Press, 1920), pp. 370–375; Browne, "Literature and Doctrine of the Ḥurūfi Sect," *Journal Royal Asiatic Society*, Jan., 1898.

determine the periods that elapsed between one manifestation and the other.

The Disappearance and Triumphal Return of al-Ḥākim:—Closely allied to the incarnational theory, and working out as a corollary from it, was the belief in the immortal character of the *Imām* in whose case "disappearance" (*ghaybah*) takes the place of death and whose final "return" (*raj'ah*) is expected so that he may lead his people in triumph to a new and happy age. When, therefore, al-Ḥākim, on that fateful day in 1020 A.D., went on his usual promenade to the Muqaṭṭam hill just outside of the city of Cairo never to return—probably because he fell a victim to a plot prearranged by his sister Sitt-al-Mulk[1]—his "admirers refused to believe in his death and began to expect his return."[2] They still hold that he is in a state of temporary occultation. History has preserved for us the names of few who on different occasions tried to impersonate the returned al-Ḥākim. In his dramatic work entitled "The Return of the Druzes," Browning tells the story of one of these impostors.

This "hidden *Imām*" idea was carefully worked out by many of the extreme Shī'ah sects prior to Druzism, and reached its most elaborate expression as a doctrine in the Ismā'īliyyah group. Its psychological basis should surely be sought in the strong but unfulfilled desires and hopes of a persecuted and depressed people (as the Shī'ah were under the Umayyads and 'Abbāsids) with the supreme ambition for a saviour-leader whose coming shall usher in for them a new era of liberty and prosperity.

This Moslem Mahdi idea was subjected to Semitic Judaeo-Christian Messianic influences on the one hand, and, in its later development, to Iranian-Mandaean influences. The case of the prophet Elijah, called throughout the Christian East "the Living One" (*al-Ḥay*), was a prototype of the ever-living *Imām*. The stories of the assumption of Moses and the ascension of Isaiah in the non-canonical literature of the Bible might have served

---

[1] Ḥamzah may have had a hand in the conspiracy. Guys, *La Nation Druse*, p. 69.

[2] Al-Qalānisi, *op. cit.*, 79–80; ibn-Khallikān, *op. cit.*, III, 7; Appendix C.

as stimuli. The expression of the "hidden *Imām*" Shī'ite doctrine[1] was a reflex of Isaiah, chapter XI. The second advent of Christ was paralleled by the "return" of the Mahdi bringing politico-religious restoration.[2]

Indo-Iranian Influences:—The problem of disentangling and sorting the different elements—labelling each Judaeo-Christian, Hellenistic or Zoroastrian—which went into the make-up of the historic Shī'ah schisms is one bristling with difficulties and uncertainties. How much did Shī'ah owe to western Neo-Platonic philosophies on the one hand, and how much to eastern Persian and Indian systems of thought on the other, is not always easy to ascertain at the present stage of research.

Modern European Semitic scholars, led by Ignacz Goldziher, have, however, been inclined to underrate the eastern influence. Certain French Persian scholars, on the other hand, such as E. Blochet and Baron Carra de Vaux[3] have tried to attribute to Persianizing influences a great many of the cardinal Shī'ah beliefs. The former scholar traces the origin of the incarnational and Mahdi idea to Zoroastrian sources, Barham Amavand being the Iranian Messiah.[4]

Further investigation will probably reveal that the Indo-Iranian influence on the rise and the development of the Shī'ah sects was greater than we now realize. That such influence was clearly recognized by early Moslem scholars is evinced by the fact that al-Baghdādi,[5] for instance, goes so far as to exclude the Bāṭiniyyah, including the Qarāmiṭah and Ismā'īliyyah, from the list of Moslem sects and to classify them under *Majūs* (Magians), *i.e.*, Zoroastrians. A tradition (*ḥadīth*) puts in the mouth of the Prophet himself the following words: "The Qadarites are the Magians of my people."[6] Besides, there is no gainsaying the fact

---

1 *Cf. e.g.* the Karbiyyah doctrine in al-Baghdādi, ed. Hitti, pp. 36–37.

2 See G. van Vloten, "Zur Abbasidengeschichte," *ZDMG*, LII, 218 *seq.*

3 *Le mahométisme, le génie sémitique et le génie aryen dans l'Islam* (Paris, 1898), p. 112.

4 E. Blochet, *op. cit.*, pp. 126 *seq.*

5 Ed. Hitti, pp. 23, 170 *seq.*

6 *Ibid.*, p. 16; al-Shahrastāni, *op. cit.*, I, 54.

that Shi'ah sprang up on Persian 'Irāqi soil, that its chief protagonists have been mostly Persian, and that until the present day it constitutes the state religion of the kingdom of Persia.

In its further development the "return" doctrine (parousia) gave rise to interesting eschatological ideas to which unbridled human fancies contributed their fantastic share. According to Druze doctrine the "return" of al-Ḥākim will result in the triumph of the Unitarian religion and the worldly reward of its adherents, who will thus become high office-holders, to the discomfiture and affliction of all infidels and apostates who are then metamorphosed into menial servants, swine and dogs.[1] This corresponds in general to the resurrection day.

Unitarians:—The Druze conception of the deity is declared by them to be one of strict and uncompromising unity. In their desire to maintain a rigid confession of unity they stripped from God all attributes (*tanzīh*) which may savor of, or lead into, polytheism (*shirk*). In Allah there are no attributes distinct from his essence. He is wise, mighty, just, &c., not by wisdom, might, justice, &c., but by his own essence. There is neither "how," "when" nor "where" about him: he is incomprehensible.

In this dogma, as in the others, the Druzes were no originators. They had for precedent that interesting semi-philosophical, semi-religious body which flourished under al-Ma'mūn and was known by the name of al-Mu'tazilah[2] and the equally interesting fraternal order of the "Brethren of Purity" (*Ikhwān al-Ṣafa*).

The Druze favorite name for themselves is *Muwaḥḥidūn*[3]—Unitarians—believers in one and only one God. In this they

---

[1] See Druze catechism in Adler, *op. cit.*, pp. 122–123; de Bock, *op. cit.*, pp. 147–148; "A Catechism of the Druzes," *Palestine Exploration Fund Quarterly Statement* (London, 1886), pp. 39–40.

[2] al-Shahrastāni, I, 55; Mas'ūdi, *Murūj al-Dhahab*, Texte et Traduction par C. Barbier de Meynard (Paris, 1871), VI, 20.

[3] The Moorish dynasty which originated with ibn-Tumart in the 12th century and conquered all northern Africa and Moslem Spain bore the same name corrupted through Spanish into "Almohades." The same name is a favorite one with the modern Wahhābis of Nejd.

follow the precedent of the Mu'tazilah who insisted on calling themselves "The People of Justice and Unity" (*Ahl al-'Adl w-al-Tawḥīd*).

III. FIVE DIVINE MINISTERS AND THREE INFERIOR ONES

The Process of Emanation:—Having accepted the Allah of the Mu'tazilah and "Brethren of Purity," already reduced to a flimsy abstraction, the Druze mind could not rest until it had personified God's mind, will, word, &c., and made separate beings out of each of them, constituting the five supreme ministers (*Ḥudūd*, literally, bounds or precepts).

The first one whom the primeval God created, and that by a process of emanation from himself,[1] was the "Universal Mind," Ḥamzah himself, the real founder of the Druze religion and its supreme pontiff who thus becomes the ruler of the universe. Even on the day of judgment he promotes and demotes whomsoever he pleases, a sort of proxy or demiurge for the divine Ḥākim. In the meantime an "Opposer" (*Ḍudd*)[2] is created by the same process of emanation, a kind of antagonist to the "Universal Mind," whose object it is to nullify the work of the Mind. This makes it necessary for God to create, by emanation from the "Universal Mind," a second minister—the "Universal Soul." This "Universal Soul" is in the position of a wife to the "Universal Mind," and from it emanates the "Word." By similar processes the "Right Wing" or "Precedent" and the "Left Wing" or "Follower" are brought into existence, the "Left Wing" being none other than al-Muqtana Bahā'-al-Dīn, the fifth and last supreme minister who stands at the head of a lower hierarchy[3] and whose multitudinous treatises and epistles, together

---

[1] For this process of creation, see *Mukhtaṣar al-Bayān fi Majra al-Zamān*, MS. (translated in part by Guys, *Théogonie des Druses*, Paris, 1863, pp. 3–84). The theory was first promulgated by Ḥamzah, *Kashf al-Haqā'iq* and in other MSS.

[2] Differently translated into "Rival" by de Sacy and Guys, and "Contrast" by Friedlaender.

[3] There was a hierarchy of missionaries graded into *Dā'i*, *Ma'dhūn*, and *Mukāsir*.

with those of Ḥamzah, form the Druze sacred literature. This Bahā'-al-Dīn may have been of Christian origin [1] as his writings reveal unusual familiarity with the New Testament and Christian liturgy. (See Appendix E.)

The Neo-Platonic Source:—We are evidently here in the atmosphere of the "emanation" theory which characterizes both Neo-Platonic [2] and Gnostic schools of philosophy and which must have filtered into the Druze system through Qarāmiṭah and "Brethren of Purity" channels. According to Professor Scott in Hastings' *Encyclopaedia of Religion and Ethics*,[3] "The first characteristic feature of Gnosticism is that at the head of the Universe stands a supreme God who is not so much a personal Deity as the abstract ground of all existence. From the supreme God there proceed a number of beings in a descending scale of dignity who are arranged in pairs, male and female."

The third minister, the "Word," is presumably an echo of the Christian Alexandrian *Logos*.

The doctrine of "Opposers," or the simultaneous revelation of the Deity in a good principle and an evil principle, parallels the Zoroastrian dualistic doctrine and reminds us of the Syzygy theory in the pseudo-Clementines.[4] The Zoroastrian influence is further shown by the reference to God as the "light" with the opposing principle as the "darkness."[5] A further working out of this same principle in the Druze system is in the case of the

[1] De Sacy, *Exposé*, I, 85, n. I. In his Epistle to Emperor Constantine and in the one entitled "Christianity," Bahā'-al-Dīn confuses John the Evangelist with John the Baptist and John Chrysostom. He identifies Ḥamzah with Christ and finds in the "three days" in which Jesus said he could rebuild the temple direct reference to Ḥamzah. He also uses parables that breathe the same atmosphere as those of the New Testament. See one of his parables in de Sacy, *Chrestomathie Arabe* (Paris, 1826), I, 304–309.

[2] See Goldziher, "Neuplatonische und gnostische Elemente im Ḥadīṯ," *Zeitschrift für Assyriologie* (1909), XXII, 317 *seq.*

[3] Article "Gnosticism."

[4] *Recognitiones*, III, 59, 61; *Homilies*, II, 15.

[5] *Cf.* Friedlaender, *Journal American Oriental Society*, XXIX, 116.

creation of the prophets where many of them have " Opposers." Adam for instance has Ḥārith ibn-Tarmāḥ against him.[1]

Like Neo-Platonism and Gnosticism, the Nuṣayriyyah assume an agent of creation, a demiurge, in the person of 'Ali. The Mufawwaḍiyyah[2] (the Believers in Entrusting) taught that God had entrusted Muḥammad with the creation and management of the universe, but Muḥammad in turn entrusted 'Ali with the task. But the " Brethren of Purity " have perhaps contributed more than any one else towards the introduction into and the formulation of the emanation-demiurge idea in Islam, and that because through their religious philosophic works,[3] which were encyclopaedic in their character, they not only gave technical expression in Arabic to the foreign concepts involved but popularized the concepts and gave the expressions currency.

Inferior Ministers:—Below the five superior ministers and standing in a subordinate position to them are three orders of minor ministers which we may term: " Propagator " (*Dā'i*), " Licensed " (*Ma'dhūn*), and " Pioneer " (*Mukāsir* or *Naqīb*).[4] Their functions are not clearly defined in the Druze manuscripts, but seem to be of the missionary type. This can be ascertained from the meaning of the Arabic names applied to them and from a study of corresponding officials in the Bāṭiniyyah system, which was one of the best and most efficiently organized systems of religious propaganda that Islam ever developed.

The " Propagator " assumes the rôle of the chief agent for the spreading of the faith. The " Licensed " has authority to preach, but is subject to the direction and guidance of the " Propagator." The " Pioneer " assumes responsibility for arousing the doubts of the would-be convert regarding his old beliefs, thus preparing him for the reception of the novel religion as soon as it is

---

[1] Ḥamzah, *al-Sīrah al-Mustaqīmah*, MS.

[2] Al-Baghdādi, ed. Hitti, p. 157.

[3] See *Rasā'il Ikhwān al-Ṣafa*, ed. F. Dieterici (*Die Abhandlungen der Ichwān eṣ-Ṣafa*, Leipzig, 1883), pp. 3–4.

[4] *Sabab al-Asbāb w-al-Kanz*, MS., also in *Le Monde Oriental* (Uppsala, 1909), vol. III, p. 100.

preached to him by a "Licensed" or a "Propagator." His office, as the Arabic name indicates, is one of breaking up and destroying.

Here again the male and female principles are represented in these ministers in their relation one to the other, and to the upper hierarchy. The "Propagator" is in the position of a wife with respect to the "*Ḥujjah*", and of a husband with respect to the "Licensed." The "Licensed" is in the position of a wife to the "Propagator," and a husband to the "Pioneer." The same double status applies to the "Pioneer."[1]

Below these inferior ministers stand the rank and file of Druze believers.

IV. THE PROPHETIC SUCCESSION

Seven Major Prophets:—Next in rank to the divine ministers in the Druze hierarchy stand the prophets. The prophetic succession tallies in general with the preceding Ismā'īliyyah series of seven.[2] Adam heads the list which includes Noah, Abraham, Moses, Jesus ('Īsa ibn-Yūsuf), Muḥammad, and Muḥammad ibn-Ismā'īl. Each one of these legislating prophets (*Nāṭiq*) has by his side a minor prophet (*Asās*) acting as a lieutenant or substitute and having under him twelve disciples (*Ḥujjah*). The substitute, also called "silent" (*Ṣāmit*), utters no new doctrine but merely teaches and develops that which he has received from his chief, the legislative prophet. The substitute represents the female and the legislator the male principles.[3] The list of substitutes includes Ishmael, Aaron, Simon and 'Ali, and that of disciples, Enoch, Daniel, Plato and other biblical and Greek characters.[4] Each "period" or "cycle" is introduced by a legislative prophet. Between one legislative prophet and the other are seven intervening *Imāms* of whom the first is in each case the trusted and intimate substitute (*Asās, Ṣāmit*) of his chief, the legislating prophet (*Nāṭiq*).

---

1 Ḥamzah, *Mīthāq al-Nisā'*, MS.

2 E. Blochet, *Le Messianisme*, *op. cit.*, p. 59.

3 Al-Tamīmi, *Taqsīm al-'Ulūm*, MS.; Ḥamzah, *Mīthāq al-Nisā'*, MS.

4 Ḥamzah, *al-Sīrah al-Mustaqīmah*, MS.

Seven a Sacred Number:—As in the case of the "periods" between the successive incarnations, so in the case of the prophetic successions, the "periods" or "cycles" are all nicely arranged and determined by cabalistic figuring in which the numbers seven and seventy,[1] as is to be expected, take a prominent place. The Pythagorean origin of this system of computation is not difficult to detect. Regarding the mystic nature of the number seven, Bahā'-al-Dīn reasons thus: "Everything when it gets to be seven ends and should be replaced by another. For example the seven days, when they end they begin over again... Also the heavens are seven, the earths are seven, the climates are seven, the height of man by his own span is seven, and the orifices in his face are seven. Likewise the legislative prophets are seven, their substitutes are seven and the intervening *Imāms* between one legislator and the other are seven."[2]

Following their spiritual ancestors, the Ismā'īliyyah, the Druzes also believe in seven heavens, seven seas, seven earths and seven hidden *Imāms*. The identification of the *Imāms* with the heavens becomes an easy step and betrays ancient Babylonian and Chaldaean astrological influences. Ismā'īl ibn-Muḥammad is identified with the first heaven; Muḥammad ibn-'Abdullāh, with the fourth; al-Ḥusayn ibn-Muḥammad, with the fifth and 'Abdullāh ibn-al-Mahdi with the seventh.[3]

Excellence of Druze System:—Each one of the Druze legislator-prophets abrogates in his turn the law of the preceding one. So did the Ismā'īliyyah prophets. The antecedent of this general idea should be sought in the abrogation by Muḥammad of the Jewish law[4] and is in harmony, though not identical, with the Marcionite Gnostic theories. As a corollary to that, the Druzes consider all former religions, including Christianity, Judaism and

---

[1] Ḥamzah, *Kashf al-Ḥaqā'iq*, MS.

[2] *Al-Juz' al-Awwal*, MS.

[3] Al-Tamīmi, *Taqsīm al-'Ulūm*, MS.; 'Abd-al-Ghaffār, *Majra al-Zamān*, MS. = Henri Guys, *Théogonie des Druses ou Abrégé de leur Système Religieux*, traduit de l'Arabe (Paris, 1863), pp. 54–55.

[4] Koran 2:286, 4:158, 7:156.

Islam as forerunners and varied types of Druzism, which supersedes and excels them all.

Adam:—Of special interest to us are Adam and Jesus who seem to stand above the other prophets and share in the divine essence. A number of Jewish Christian sects, such as the Essenes and Nazarenes, adopted this gnostic view, which, combined with Persian and old Babylonian mythology, furnished Mani with the doctrine of the original man. The Adam of the Druze theology, therefore, is not exactly the Adam of Genesis but the "original man"[1] of the Manichaeans, the *Adam Kadmon*[2] of the Jewish cabala.

Certain Moslem sects, like the Muḥammadiyyah, went so far as to declare the divinity of Adam.

Jesus:—The Jesus ('Īsa ibn-Yūsuf) of the Druze manuscripts is also somewhat different from the Jesus of the New Testament. He is rather the Moslem Jesus patterned after the conception of him by the ancient heretic sect of the Docetae who held that Christ suffered only in appearance. This doctrine was handed down to the Moslems probably through Manichaean channels.[3] The Manichaean movement, which arose in close connection with Mandaeanism in 'Irāq or southern Babylonia, about the middle of the third century A.D., and which, as *al-Fihrist* declares, was a blend of the old Magian cult with Christianity,[4] was Iranian in its mythology and cosmological beliefs. It exercised a great influence over the Moslem sects in al-'Irāq, which was also rich in Jewish and Christian sects and heresies.

---

1 "*Insān Qadīm*" in *al-Fihrist*, ed. G. Flügel (Leipzig, 1872), p. 329. See also Flügel, *Mani* (Leipzig, 1862), pp. 97, 105.

2 Louis Ginzberg, article "Adam Kadmon," *Jewish Encyclopaedia*.

3 F. C. Burkitt, *The Religion of the Manichees* (Cambridge University Press, 1925), pp. 38–40; Flügel, *Mani*, pp. 337–338.

4 *Al-Fihrist*, p. 328. That Islam knew a great deal about Mani and Manichaeanism is evidenced by the fact that our oldest and most trustworthy sources on that movement are to be found in Arabic-Moslem literature and particularly *al-Fihrist*. A peculiar sect of Manichaeanism, Mazdakiyyah, seems to have exercised tremendous influence over the Moslem sects. Al-Shahrastāni (II, 29) informs us that the Bāṭiniyyah and Qarāmiṭah in al-'Irāq were called "Mazdakites."

V. THE INNER MEANING

The Bāṭiniyyah:—Having deviated from the letter as well as from the word of Allah as revealed in the Koran, and without seeming to abrogate altogether its legislative precepts, certain schools of thought, designated by orthodox theologians Bāṭiniyyah, found it expedient to resort to a new and ingenious device—that of interpreting the religious facts esoterically or allegorically. Though classified by al-Baghdādi, al-Shahrastāni and ibn-Ḥazm as "sects," the Bāṭiniyyah were rather unorganized philosophical schools of thought. They belonged in the main to the Qarāmiṭah and Ismā'īliyyah sects, from which Druzism sprang, and to certain Ṣūfi fraternities. Truth, according to the cardinal Bāṭiniyyah concept, is to be ascertained by the discovery of an inner meaning (*bāṭin*, hence the appellation Bāṭiniyyah = Innerites) of which the outer form is a mere veil intended to keep the truth from the eyes of the uninitiate.

This device put at once into the hands of the Shī'ah schismatic sects a powerful weapon which dealt deadly blows to the core of Islam leaving only its outside shell. The shadow was there but the substance had gone. Meanwhile it enabled its adepts to appropriate from non-Moslem sources whatever suited their own convenience.

Thus through Ṣūfi and Shī'ah channels, Druzism was made to enter into the inheritance of Philo and early esoteric exegetes.

Darazi, one of the founders of the Druze system—if system it could be called—was a Bāṭini missionary, as we are told by many of his biographers.[1]

The Muḥammadan Law Abrogated:—Between unbridled allegorical interpretation of the law and its virtual suspension lies one short step, and that step was actually taken by Ḥamzah, the real founder of the Druze religion. Following the Ismā'īliyyah precedent, Ḥamzah, in his *Kitāb al-Naqḍ al-Khafi*, went so far as to abolish the so-called five pillars of Islam, including fasting,

---

[1] Ibn-Taghri-Birdi, *op. cit.*, p. 69.

pilgrimage and almsgiving, and substituted for them four articles of faith relating to the knowledge of God, of Ḥamzah, the ministers, and the seven moral precepts.[1] These precepts enjoin the love of truth in speech, watching over one another's safety, renouncing other religions, recognizing the existence in all ages of the principle of divine unity in al-Ḥākim and acquiescing in his actions whatever they be.[2]

On account of this, orthodox Islam never hesitated to exclude Druzism from its fold. In fact certain conservative canonists, like the puritan ibn-Taymiyyah (1263–1328 A.D.), whose legal system greatly influenced the rise of the Wahhābi movement in Nejd, went so far as to express a religious opinion (*fatwa*) favoring "warring against the Druzes as a more meritorious duty than warring against the Armenians, because the former are included in the Moslem territory but are not of it." [3]

The Mystic Element:—Akin to the esoteric conception of the scriptures is the principle of mysticism which found its highest expression in Islam in the Ṣūfi movement and traces of which are prominent in the Druze initiate view of life. Ṣūfism began as asceticism, became in succession mystical and theosophical, and finally advanced to extreme pantheism. The four principal sources of Ṣūfism are Christianity, Neo-Platonism, Gnosticism and Buddhism. The Neo-Platonic character of Moslem Ṣūfism has been rendered clear by the contributions of two English scholars, E. G. Browne and R. A. Nicholson. It would, however, be a mistake to ignore entirely the influence of the Buddhist view upon the later development of historic Ṣūfism, especially after Islam had spread eastward to the confines of China and brought Indian thought within its horizon. The encyclopaedic author of *al-Fihrist*[4] († 996) quotes at some length from an archaic version

---

[1] See Ḥamzah, *Mīthāq al-Nisā'*, MS.

[2] These precepts occur in many Druze MSS. See *infra*, p. 51. Bahā'-al-Dīn devotes one tract to each one of them. *Cf.* Guys, *Théogonie*, *op. cit.*, pp. 77–84.

[3] Al-'Umari, *al-Ta'rīf bi-al-Muṣṭalaḥ al-Sharīf* (Cairo, 1312 A.H.); *Cf.* al-Qalqashandi, *Ṣubḥ al-A'sha* (Cairo, 1918), XIII, 248–249.

[4] *Op. cit.*, p. 347.

of a Buddhist book. The monumental piece of Arabic literature *al-Aghānī*[1] has left us at least one portrayal of an unmistakable Buddhistic view of life. And the *Zindīq* monks, described by al-Jāḥiẓ,[2] were, according to Goldziher, "Either Indian Sadhus, or Buddhist monks or at least their imitators."[3] Under Indian influence the pantheistic idea in Ṣūfi Islam becomes more apparent.

Sheikhs:—The Druzes share with their intellectual ancestors —the Ṣūfis, Ismā'īliyyah and Qarāmiṭah—both the esoteric interpretation of the law and the mystical outlook on life. Their community is divided into '*Uqqāl*, initiate, intelligent, spiritual; and *Juhhāl*, uninitiate, ignorant, worldly. A course *ṣūf*[4] (wool) outer garment is the distinguishing dress of the former, among whom the most meritorious *Ajāwīd* lead an almost ascetic life.

The '*Uqqāl* are also called "*Sheikhs*,"[5] an Arabic word connoting old age, seniority and respect. This word has in recent years been introduced into the English language and corrupted in both pronunciation and meaning.

To the high rank of enlightened '*Uqqāl*, no one can aspire whose character has not marked him out as one entirely trustworthy and capable of extreme secrecy. Before admission, however, he must be subjected to a rigorous process of long trial and probation. Then follows the ceremonial rite of induction. This secret ceremony has been witnessed and described by only one or two outsiders throughout the whole history of the Druze religion.

---

[1] Cairo edition (20 vols.), III, 24—*Sumniyyah* is the term applied to the Indian sects which influenced many Moslems.

[2] *Kitāb al-Ḥayawān* (Cairo, 1323 A.H.), IV, 146–147.

[3] *Vorlesungen*, *op. cit.*, p. 160.

[4] For the origin of the word "Ṣūfi" from *ṣūf* = wool, see Nöldeke in *ZDMG*, XLVII, 47.

[5] The middle vowel is pronounced long like "i" in "bite," and the final "kh" is guttural, something like the German "ch." *Cf.* "Usi e Credenze dei Drusi" in *Oriente Moderno* (Rome, 1925), V, pp. 469–472.

Once admitted to the favored rank, the Sheikh begins to wear a heavy white turban, and abstains from gaudy colors, swearing and obscene language. His deportment becomes dignified and reserved. Under no condition is he thereafter to touch alcoholic liquor or to smoke. He may even refrain from eating at the table of a wealthy man or government official lest something of the money used in buying the food might have been illegitimately acquired.

CHAPTER VI

DOGMAS AND PRECEPTS

I. TRANSMIGRATION OF SOULS

The Druze belief in metempsychosis is very popular and strong and, in contrast to their other beliefs, is professed openly by the believers. The writer's impression of stories told him by schoolmates in the Lebanon regarding newly-born children who made utterances involving memories of former incarnations is still vivid and clear in his mind. A story that found great circulation in the local press of Syria in the last few months relates how a Druze leader in one of the recent raids against the French stood on a bridge at Wādi-al-Taym and declared to his men that some fifty years ago he was killed on that same spot where he was this time leading his men.[1]

Method of Operation:—According to the learned Druze doctrine, the principle of transmigration of souls operates only from one human body to another. All souls were created at once from the "light of Ḥamzah" and their actual number is "neither increased by births nor decreased by deaths."[2] The ignorant among them, however, hold popular beliefs involving reincarnation in animal forms, and that probably explains the erroneous statements made by many writers, including the statement in the *Encyclopaedia of Islam*,[3] to the effect that they believe that the wicked return in bodies of dogs.

---

1 *Al-Machriq* (Beirūt), June, 1926. For another story see I. J. Nakhlah, *Ḥall al-Rumūz fi Mu'taqad al-Durūz* (Cairo, 1897), p. 38.

2 Bahā'-al-Dīn, *Tamyīz al-Muwaḥḥidīn al-Ṭā'i'in*, MS.

3 Article "Druzes" by Baron Carra de Vaux. The same mistake is made by William Ewing, *Arab and Druze at Home* (London, 1907), p. 88. *Cf.* F. J. Bliss, *The Religions of Modern Syria and Palestine* (New York, 1912), p. 308; and J. T. Parfit, *Druzes and the Secret Sects of Syria* (Westminster, 1917), p. 26, *Among the Druzes of Lebanon and Bashan* (London, 1917), pp. 235–236; Ḥanna abi-Rāshid, *Jabal al-Durūz* (Cairo, 1925), p. 44.

In his epistle refuting the arguments of the Nuṣayri,[1] Ḥamzah utterly rejects the doctrine of transmigration, stating that "if anyone believes in it as the Nuṣayriyyah do, he loses both this and the next world." The Druze catechism, formulated long after the days of Bahā'-al-Dīn and Ḥamzah, teaches that the infidels and apostates are metamorphosed into dogs and swine[2] as well as menial servants.

Earlier Moslem Sects Believing in Transmigration:—That the Druzes had within the fold of Islam various precursors in the doctrine of metempsychosis is demonstrated by the fact that al-Baghdādi[3] and ibn-al-Jawzi[4] each devote a whole chapter to *Aṣḥāb al-Tanāsukh*, *i.e.*, the believers in transmigration. Ibn-Ḥazm,[5] al-Shahrastāni,[6] and al-Maqrīzi[7] have many references to such sects, chief among which stood al-Kaysāniyyah, and al-Ḥā'iṭiyyah. Stories intended to show the amusing possibilities of return in form of animals are recorded in various books of Arabic literature.

One of the most popular of these stories is that related of al-Sayyid al-Ḥimyari who believed in transmigration. A certain man came and asked him for a loan of money promising to repay it on his (debtor's) return to life. "Well," said al-Sayyid, "but even more than that, you should offer a guarantee that you will return in the form of a man." "How else can I return?" asked the would-be debtor. "I am afraid," retorted the shrewd Sayyid, "that you will return as a dog or pig, and my money will then be lost!"[8]

---

1 *Al-Radd 'Ala al-Risālah al-Dāmighah li-al-Fāsiq*, MS.

2 See the translation of "A Catechism of the Druze Religion" in *Palestine Exploration Fund Quarterly Statement* (London, 1886), pp. 39–40.

3 Ed. Hitti, pp. 164–165. See also al-Baghdādi, *al-Farq bayn al-Firaq* ed. Badr, pp. 253–259.

4 *Op. cit.*, pp. 85–86. 5 *Op. cit.*, IV, 182. 6 *Op. cit.*, II, 12.

7 *Al-Khiṭaṭ* (Cairo, 1853), II, 347, 352, 354.

8 *Al-Aghāni*, VII, 8; al-Kutubi, *Fawāt al-Wafayāt* (Cairo, 1866), I, 25. See also al-Jāḥiẓ, *Kitāb al-Ḥayawān*, VI, 24; ibn-al-Jawzi, p. 86; *Alf Laylah wa-Laylah* (Catholic Press, Beirūt), I, 41; al-Ma'arri, "Risālatu'l-Ghufrān," *Journal Royal Asiatic Society* (1902), XXXIV, 354–355 and 840.

The Manichaean doctrine of the soul, and of its lot hereafter, recognized a division of mankind into three classes: Elect, Hearers and Sinners; the Elect alone being exempt from retribution through rebirth in some lower form.[1]

When carried to its logical conclusion, as in the case of the Druze philosophy, the doctrine of transmigration dispenses altogether with the necessity for paradise and hell and takes the place of a final judgment. The time of the triumphal " return " of al-Ḥākim and the complete victory of his Unitarian religion, resulting in awarding high worldly offices to the faithful and punishing the renegades and unbelievers by assigning them to hard and menial labor, corresponds to the resurrection day.

Relation to China:—Whether this Moslem belief is of Western Pythagorean or of Eastern Indian origin is hard to ascertain, with the balance of evidence in favor of the East. Ibn-al-Jawzi[2] states that it appeared first " in the days of the Pharaoh of Moses," which is correct if taken to mean that it was of ultimate Egyptian origin. Al-Shahrastāni[3] declares that the Moslem heterodoxies received this teaching from the Mazdakian Magians, Brahman Indians, the philosophers, and Mandaeans.[4]

In the case of the Druzes, to whom China seems to be a sort of a heaven, the eastern source has evidently impressed itself strongly upon the popular imagination. When a good Druze is dead in the Lebanon, he is supposed to be reborn in China. The writer remembers hearing more than once at Druze funerals the chorus of a song which ran as this: " Happy are the people of China at the hour of your arrival! " (*Niyyāl ahl al-Ṣīn sa'at waṣltak*). The Druzes have always been conscious of the fact

---

[1] A. V. Williams Jackson, " The Doctrine of Metempsychosis in Manichaeism," *Journal American Oriental Society*, Sept., 1925, pp. 247 and 268; Burkitt, *op. cit.*, pp. 63–65.

[2] *Op. cit.*, p. 85.

[3] *Op. cit.*, II, 12.

[4] *Al-Ṣābi'ah* in Arabic mentioned in the Koran three times (2:59, 5:73, 22:17) where with the Jews and Christians they were assured religious tolerance. " The philosophers " referred to are undoubtedly the Hellenistic philosophers.

that people in the Far East hold the same views regarding the transmigration of souls.[1]

It is interesting to note in this connection that Benjamin of Tudela[2] calls the inhabitants of Khandy (Ceylon) by the same name as the people around Sidon—Druzes. He was probably impressed by the similarity of belief in transmigration among the two peoples and concluded that they must have been the same.

II. PREDESTINATION AND DISSIMULATION

In the theory of predestination, the Druzes follow in the footsteps of the Jabriyyah school of Islamic thought as opposed to the Qadariyyah.[3] The problem of reconciling the Almightiness of Allah with the free-will of man was the very first rock over which dogmatic Islam split, these two sects constituting the earliest dogmatic schism in Islam.

The Koran abounds in passages the interpretation of which favors a predestination philosophy of life. Sūrah 3, verses 26–27 reads: "Say, O God, master of the universe, thou bestowest the rule upon whom thou wilt, and thou takest away the rule from whom thou wilt; thou exaltest whomsoever thou wilt, and thou humblest whomsoever thou wilt. In thy hand is all good, for thou art all-powerful. Thou causest the night to succeed the day, and thou causest the day to succeed the night. Thou bringest forth the living out of the dead, and thou bringest forth the dead out of the living. And thou providest sustenance to whom thou wilt, without measure."

Shī'ite Contribution:—The ethical principle of dissimulation (*taqiyyah*), practiced to the present day by the Druzes, was a fundamental tenet of Shī'ah, to which the partisans of 'Ali had resort as a result of the handicaps and persecutions to which they were subjected by orthodox (Sunni) Islam during both the

---

[1] Mr. Kisbāny suggests the possibility that the use of "Ṣīn" in this connection is an esoteric one of the ancient Babylonian word *sin* for moon.

[2] *Travels* (London, 1848), p. 115.

[3] D. B. Macdonald, *Muslim Theology*, *op. cit.*, pp. 127–137.

Umayyad and 'Abbāsid periods. The theory is an old one in Islam, based upon the Koran, 3 : 28–29: "Let not the believers choose the infidels for protectors in preference to other believers. He who doth this hath no claim upon Allah, unless he doth it in dissimulation (*taqiyyah*) and for protection... Whether ye conceal what is in your breasts, or whether ye proclaim it, Allah knoweth it, for he knoweth whatever is in the heavens and whatever is on earth." The Khārijites, antedating the Shī'ah, recognized its legitimacy. The Shī'ite contribution to it consisted of the point that when a believer is in a place where his adversaries are in the ascendancy, not only *may* he profess outwardly the form of the prevailing religion but he *must* do so in order to protect himself and his coreligionists.[1]

The historical illustration of this principle, as it worked out in the case of the Druzes, took place in the thirties of the last century when the Egyptian Ibrāhīm Pasha insisted on enforcing his conscription laws and many Druzes, in order to evade the draft, began to patronize the Christian churches of their Maronite neighbors. A few years ago when the great Druze leader, al-Amīr Muṣṭafa Arislān, who had held many high governmental positions under the Turks, died, his funeral services were conducted according to the Sunni Moslem rites.

This principle must have attached itself to more than one of the secret religions in pre-Islamic days. It has its modern applications in the case of the Persian and Syrian Bahā'is, the Domneh Jews of Salonika (of whom the famous Turkish minister Djevīd Bey is supposed to have been one), and the Stavriote[2] Greeks of Asia Minor who after the proclamation of the constitution in 1908 put off the Moslem garb and reasserted their Christianity which they had practiced in hiding.

---

[1] Goldziher, *Le dogme et la loi*, trans. Félix Arin (Paris, 1920), pp. 169–170. See also *ZDMG*, *op. cit.*, LX, 213 *seq.*

[2] These crypto-Christian Greeks are called in the Levant "Mezzo-Mezzos." Leon Dominian, *Frontiers of Language and Nationality in Europe* (New York, 1917), p. 277.

III. THE CULT OF THE CALF

The Fact:—Persistent local rumor continues to associate "calf worship" with the Druze religion, but the Druzes themselves have with equal persistence and vehemence denied it. No worse curse could even today be levelled against a Druze in the Lebanon than to call him "calf worshiper." Certain travelers like Pococke[1] gave credence to the report; others including Volney[2] rejected it. That there is jealously guarded and hidden from the uninitiate eye, in one of their leading places of seclusion (*khalwah*), of which there are about forty in the Lebanon,[3] some gold figure of a calf or bull inside of a silver box has been almost ascertained beyond doubt. A high Druze sheikh has practically admitted in a recent interview the existence of such a box.[4] Paul Casanova reports in the *Revue archéologique*[5] the discovery of a baked clay figure of a ram or sheep with the name of al-Ḥākim inscribed on it. Passages in the tracts of Ḥamzah[6] and Bahā'-al-Dīn[7] referring in a derogatory manner to the "calf" and the "worshipers of the calf" are not lacking, but one passage in the epistle entitled *al-Asrār* (Secrets or Mysteries) has clear and unmistakable reference to "the box in which is the figure of the incarnation of our Lord."[8]

Its Interpretation:—The question, in view of the secrecy that surrounds the cult and the ambiguity of some of the references, is one of interpretation. De Sacy[9] explains the calf as the emblem of *Iblīs* (devil), the enemy and rival of al-Ḥākim. Colonel

---

[1] *A Description of the East*, *op. cit.*, p. 94.

[2] Volney, *Voyage en Égypte et en Syrie* (Paris, 1825) (*Œuvres*, t. II), p. 409.

[3] Article "Durūz," *Dā'irat al-Ma'ārif*, ed. B. Bustāny (Beirūt, 1876–1900).

[4] W. B. Seabrook, "The Golden Calf of the Druzes," *Asia* (New York), March, 1926. See also *Revue de l'Orient*, X, 238.

[5] Year 1891, "Figurine en terre cuite avec inscription arabe." See also Blochet, *Le Messianisme*, *op. cit.*, p. 98, n. 1.

[6] *Al-Ghāyah w-al-Naṣīḥah*, MS. In *al-Sīrah al-Mustaqīmah*, MS., the statement is made that in Plato's (*Iflāṭūn*) legislation there was no "calf worship."

[7] *Risālat al-Wādi*, MS.

[8] This epistle is printed in part in Adler, *op. cit.*, p. 136.

[9] *Exposé*, *op. cit.*, II, 235.

Churchill states that Ḥamzah, indignant at the treachery of his emissary, Darazi, denounced him as the "calf whom a deluded people had set up as their idol."[1] Lieut.-Col. Conder considers it "a relic of older paganism" which they keep in their solitary meeting places "only to treat with insult and contempt."[2]

If and when the calf cult is proved in the case of the Druze religion, some connection will then be sought with earlier cognate Israelitish and Egyptian cults. Animal worship has greatly figured in Oriental religions, and Christianity bears traces of its survival.

IV. SEVEN PRECEPTS OF ḤAMZAH

Eight Dogmas:—The chief dogmas of Druze belief, which we have hitherto tried to analyze and trace back to Moslem, Christian, Jewish, Neo-Platonic and Manichaean ancestry can be summed up under eight main formulas.

The first dogma is the confession of the unity of God. The second is the belief in successive manifestations of the deity in human form. The third is the acceptance of al-Ḥākim as the last and greatest of these divine incarnations. The fourth is the recognition of the five superior ministers who partake of the divine essence. The fifth is the consideration of Ḥamzah, the first minister, as the supreme ruler of the age (*Wali-al-Zamān*). The sixth is the belief in the philosophic concept of predestination. The seventh is the belief in the transmigration of souls. The eighth is the observance of the seven precepts of Ḥamzah who, on behalf of al-Ḥākim, absolved his followers from the obligations of Islam and instituted these new precepts for them.

The obligations of Islam, the so-called "five pillars," are: the testimony that God is one and that Muḥammad is his apostle, fasting, prayer, pilgrimage, and almsgiving. No one who does not practice these five can have any claim on orthodox Islam.

---

[1] Charles H. Churchill, *The Druzes and Maronites under the Turkish Rule* (London, 1862), p. 12.

[2] *The Latin Kingdom of Jerusalem, op. cit.*, p. 234.

Ḥamzah's Precepts:—The first precept of Ḥamzah enjoins veracity in speech; the second, protection and mutual aid to the brethren in faith; the third, renunciation of all forms of former worship and false belief; the fourth, repudiation of the devil (*Iblīs*) and all forces of evil; the fifth, confession of the unity of the Ḥākim-God; the sixth, acquiescence in his acts no matter what they be; and the seventh, absolute submission and resignation to his divine will in both secret and public.[1]

Sources and Operation:—The first two precepts enunciated by the founder of Druzism are ethical in their nature and therefore difficult to trace back to their origin. The genealogy of the third and fourth is likewise difficult to ascertain. The fifth is the dogma we treated before, and the rest are corollaries from that dogma. The operation of the first precept is, of course, circumscribed by the already established law of dissimulation.

Of these principles the second has perhaps been the most potent force in the life and history of the Druze people. It has made of the Druze community one compact social body, presenting more the aspects of a religious fraternal order than a sect. This fraternal feature is one of the distinctive characteristics of the Druze people and has, in a large measure, contributed to their survival to the present day. It has enabled them at the time of crisis to act in unison and as one body moved primarily by motives of self-interest and by the instinct of self-preservation.

---

[1] These precepts occur in most of their leading religious tracts.

CHAPTER VII

FOLKLORE

Animism and Saint Worship:—With the semi-, or quasi-, religious popular beliefs held by the Druzes of today which do not figure in their books and learned system—if indeed system it be—we are not particularly concerned in this study. Such beliefs represent, in general, animistic, pantheistic and polytheistic remnants of ancient beliefs which those people held before their admission into, and profession of, Islam. Many of them, under some form or other, are shared by their neighbors, Christian and Moslem alike. The belief in magic and in the evil eye is potent and widespread.

A venerable oak-tree in 'Ālayh, Lebanon, by which I passed many times, was ordinarily so bedecked with colorful rags from the clothes of pious Druze passers-by that its fame spread throughout the land under the name of "The Mother-of-Rags Oak-Tree."

The sight of Druze men and women walking a distance of miles, barefoot, to visit some *wali* tomb, particularly that of al-Sayyid 'Abdullāh al-Tanūkhi in 'Abayh,[1] is familiar to all those who have lived for any length of time in south Lebanon. This cult of the dead, a form of polytheism, is strong among them as it is among other Eastern peoples.[2]

Charges of Licentious Practices:—Ever since the days of the Nuṣayri, whose charges of immorality against the Druzes solicited a special reply from Ḥamzah,[3] and the days of Benjamin of Tudela

---

[1] See Appendix F.

[2] For other illustrations of the folklore, see "Druzes" in *Palestine Exploration Fund Quarterly Statement*, 1889, pp. 120–126.

[3] *Al-Radd 'ala al-Risālah al-Dāmighah li-al-Fāsiq al-Nuṣayri*, MS.

who visited the Lebanon around 1165 A.D. and wrote that the Druzes "live incestuously" and once every year assemble and "hold promiscuous intercourse,"[1] similar charges have been brought against them, as they are against most secret cults, without much to substantiate them. There is, however, more to justify charges of nocturnal orgies and phallic worship against the Nuṣayriyyah of Syria and the 'Ali-Ilāhis of Lūristān.[2]

The secrecy with which the Druzes hold their Thursday evening meetings in their secluded *khalwahs*, which meetings are attended also by the initiated women sitting behind a partition, has undoubtedly contributed to the rise of such suspicions. The *khalwahs* usually crown the hilltops, and the meetings consist principally of the perusal and explanation of the sacred writings, some of which are chanted. The writings of Ḥamzah and Bahā'-al-Dīn, together with the commentaries of al-Sayyid 'Abdullāh, constitute the favorite readings. The early part of certain sessions is open for the uninitiated Druzes. The latter part of the evening is usually consumed with political and social discussions.

Ḥamzites versus Darazites:—Nevertheless, it is admitted by the Druzes themselves that Darazi, the disreputed missionary whose name the Druzes reluctantly bear, in order to swell the ranks of his converts did sanction some licentious and libertine principles. But he was later discredited and deposed by his superior Ḥamzah from the position he aspired to maintain as the head of the Druze religion.[3] The liberties introduced by Darazi were evidently too seducing in their appeal to be entirely abandoned and to this day the line of cleavage between the purer

---

[1] *Early Travels in Palestine ... Travels of Rabbi Benjamin of Tudela* (London, 1848), p. 80. This "*fête des bougies*" is described by "St. Ed." in *Revue de l'Orient*, 2e sér. (Paris, 1841), IV, 140.

[2] Sir Henry Layard, *Early Adventures in Persia, Susiana, and Babylonia* (London, 1887), I, 217 and II, 318; C. R. Conder, *Syrian Stone-Lore* (London, 1896), p. 423.

[3] Ḥamzah denounces him bitterly in a tract entitled *al-Ghāyah w-al-Naṣīḥah*, MS.

and more orthodox Ḥamzites and the Darazites is noticeable. In the introduction of his unscrupulous libertinism, Darazi was following the precedent of the Qarāmiṭah,[1] sometimes called the "free-lovers" and the "Bolsheviks of Islam."

Family Organization:—In their family life, the Druzes, under Christian influence, strictly adhere to the monogamous form of organization; but divorce is easy. The *Encyclopaedia of Islam*,[2] probably misled by Volney,[3] erroneously states that they allow polygamy. They intermarry among themselves only.

* * *

Summary and Conclusion:—On the whole it might be said that the immediate origins of the Druze religion should be sought in the multitudinous heterodoxies of the Shī'ah and schools of thought which split early Islam asunder, and the ultimate origins in Neo-Platonism, Gnosticism and Manichaeism. What makes its study especially interesting and valuable[4] is the fact that while most of those systems from which the eclectic Druze founders drew their material have perished and become extinct, the Druze religion is still virile and strong and its followers are today numerous and aggressive enough to attract international attention.

---

[1] Al-Baghdādi, ed. Hitti, pp. 175–176, 180. According to the same authority the Khārijite Maymūniyyah (p. 169) sanctioned the marriage of grandchildren to grandparents, and nieces to uncles.

[2] Article "Druzes."

[3] *Op. cit.*, I, 425.

[4] Gibbon, *Decline and Fall of the Roman Empire, op. cit.*, chap. LVII, n. 68, states with regard to this religion that "The little that is, or deserves to be, known may be seen in the industrious Niebuhr, and the second volume of the recent and instructive *Travels* of M. de Volney."

APPENDICES

CONTAINING EXTRACTS FROM THE DRUZE SACRED WRITINGS

Appendix A

COVENANT OF INDUCTION INTO THE RELIGION OF THE RULER OF THE AGE

(MĪTHĀQ WALI-AL-ZAMĀN)

My trust I lay in our lord al-Ḥākim, the only one, the unique, the eternal; he who is above duplication and number.

So and so the son of so and so, being sound in mind and body, and out of his own free will and accord, without duress and constraint, confesses, in a way that makes it binding upon himself and can be used as a testimony against his soul, that he has hereby renounced all sects, doctrines, religions and beliefs—no matter what their character may be; that he now recognizes nothing but obedience to our lord al-Ḥākim (may the mention of his name be glorified!), obedience being adoration; that he shall not include in his worship anyone else, past, present or expected; that he has surrendered his soul, his body, his possessions, his children and everything he owns to our lord al-Ḥākim (may the mention of his name be glorified!); and that he has acquiesced in all his decisions—be they for or against him—without objecting to, or disapproving of, any of his [al-Ḥākim's] actions, whether they be pleasing or displeasing to him. In case he forsakes the religion of our lord al-Ḥākim, to which he submits by this writing and which he holds as a witness against his soul, or uses it as a cover for some other religion, or disobeys any of its commandments, then he is no more entitled to the protection of the Creator the adored, and is deprived of all the advantages bestowed by the ministers [of the Unitarian religion], and merits the chastisement meted out by al-Bār[1] the exalted (may the mention of his name be glorified!).

---

[1] One of the honorific titles of al-Ḥākim. See *supra*, p. 20.

Whoso confesses that to him there is no god in heaven worthy of adoration, and no *imām* on earth in a state of existence other than our lord al-Ḥākim (may the mention of his name be glorified!), becomes one of the victorious Unitarians.

Written in such a month of such a year of the era of the servant of our Lord[1] (may the mention of his name be glorified!) and of his slave, Ḥamzah ibn-'Ali ibn-Aḥmad, he who guides those who respond, and wreaks vengeance on the polytheists and apostates by means of the sword of our Lord (may the mention of his name be glorified!) and by the great force of his power alone.

---

[1] Al-Ḥākim is the Lord, and Ḥamzah is his servant.

Appendix B

AL-ḤĀKIM'S ORDINANCE PROHIBITING THE USE OF WINE

In the name of Allah, the compassionate, the merciful.

Praise be to Allah who has rendered Islam strong and dear through its pious saints, and has entrusted its laws to the *imāms* of his religion and to his blessed confidants who have preserved them! And may Allah's grace be upon our grandfather Muḥammad, the seal of the prophets and the chief of all messengers—may Allah's grace be upon him and upon all members of his holy family!

The Commander of the Believers, duly authorized by Allah and entrusted by him with the management of the affairs of both religion and state over which his word is supreme, is devoting all his energy, judgment, and deliberations to defend these two institutions, to guard them against any damage that may find its way into them, to promote their interests and welfare, to strengthen the agencies that make firm their foundations, to give preference to whatsoever maintains their organization, and to preserve whatever alterations and modifications have been introduced for their perfection and completion. Allah (may he remain majestic and glorious!) accords his support to the Commander of the Believers in all that conforms to his favor, and enables him to succeed in accomplishing whatever makes him merit his favor and pleasure and deserve his grace and his power.

Verily the measure that will produce the most useful results to Islam and the Moslems, and that will contribute more than any other measure to the maintenance of the fundamentals of our religion, is to declare a general prohibition for everybody against the use of intoxicating liquor, and to deny them the right of insisting upon the drinking of intoxicating liquor which is the center of all sorts of evil and the conductor to all kinds of detestable and abhorrent acts.

The Commander of the Believers has therefore ordained, expecting from Allah success, that this edict be written so that it be read to the privileged classes as well as to the common people, whether they be high in rank or low, making illegal the use of any kind of intoxicating liquor, no matter what its brand, name, color or taste may be (liquor being used here to include every kind of drink, whether it be intoxicating in large or in small quantities), and prohibiting all resort to the sayings and opinions justifying its use together with all interpretations and excuses which the rabble hold fast to; for the Commander of the Believers has declared all that illegal, after having heard all things connected with it. He has prohibited the use of intoxicating liquor, its purchase, storage, manufacture, and extraction to the end that the whole empire may be purified of its evil effects.

The execution of this edict he has left as a trust in the hands of those of his officials who are ever loyal to him, and as a sign of allegiance in charge of his counsellors and those who are faithful to him, holding them responsible for investigating all cases and submitting full reports regarding their findings. The Commander of the Believers himself has thus become discharged before Allah of all responsibility and evil consequence in this world and in the next.

Let all the godly, the believers, and those included within the fold of true religion know that this is issued by the Commander of the Believers; and let them do accordingly. Let them unhesitatingly obey its command and beware of violating it; for the Commander of the Believers has prepared for the enemies of his ordinance painful punishment and shameful degradation.

And Allah alone is all-sufficient to the Commander of the Believers and the best one to depend upon.

Written in the month of Dhu-al-Qa'dah, 400.

Praise be to Allah alone, and may his grace be upon his Messenger, the seal of the prophets, as well as upon his holy family; and may he give them peace!

Appendix C

EXCERPT FROM THE CHARTER FOUND POSTED ON THE WALLS OF THE MOSQUES ON THE OCCASION OF THE DISAPPEARANCE OF OUR LORD AL-IMĀM AL-ḤĀKIM

The friend of Allah, the Commander of the Believers, has at last abandoned all mortals to themselves wandering in their desert and in their state of blindness which they had preferred to guidance—just as Moses had abandoned his people—until perdition came near attacking them while they were unaware. He made his exit from their midst while they were in a state of doubt regarding him, disagreeing among themselves and faltering between different opinions, neither rendering obedience to truth nor returning to the friend of Allah. Allah has said: "But if they had referred it to Allah, to his Apostle and to those in authority among them, it would have become clear to those of them who fail to understand it."[1]

O you people! The word of Allah (may he remain high!) is the most eloquent preacher, and what is clear from this sermon to you is your poverty and your need for the pardon of Allah (may he remain high!) and the pardon of his friend, the Commander of the Believers, upon whom Allah's peace is more abundant than upon you. Oblivion leads to negligence, negligence leads to rebellion, and rebellion leads to perdition. For Allah (may his name remain blessed and high!) has said: "But if they, having wronged themselves had come to thee asking Allah's forgiveness, and if the Apostle had asked forgiveness for them, they would surely have found Allah a for-

[1] *Cf.* Koran 4 : 85.

giving and merciful one."[1] The greatest of all sayers [Allah] has also said: "Excepting those who shall repent and believe and do righteous works,"[2] "for verily Allah loveth those who seek his indulgence and loveth those who wish to purify themselves."[3] Allah (may he remain blessed and high!) has moreover said: "And when my worshipers ask thee concerning me, [say] I am nigh unto them, ready to answer the supplication of him that calleth, when he calleth unto me."[4]

Hasten, therefore, hasten, O you people! If you stand upon a desolate tract of land, then your eyes shall be directed towards the first road[5] which was pursued by the Commander of the Believers (may Allah's peace be upon him!) when he disappeared. Assemble there, yourselves and your children, purify your hearts and make your intentions sincere toward Allah, the Lord of the universe. Repent before him in a true manner and beseech him by the best methods of supplication leading to pardon and forgiveness, so that he may show mercy to you by according you the return of his friend, and may turn his heart in compassion toward you; for he is mercy unto you and unto all his creation in accordance with what Allah (may he remain blessed and high!) has said to his Messenger [Muḥammad] (may Allah's grace be upon him and upon his kin!): "We have not sent thee other than as mercy unto all creatures."[6]

But beware, beware lest any of you should try to trace the steps of the Commander of the Believers (may Allah's blessing be upon him!), or should attempt to discover any information whatsoever![7] Cease not at the beginning of the road to reiterate

---

[1] Koran 4 : 67.

[2] *Ibid.* 25 : 70.

[3] *Ibid.* 2 : 222.

[4] *Ibid.* 2 : 182.

[5] This is the road leading outside of Cairo toward al-Muqaṭṭam and which al-Ḥākim followed when he took his usual evening promenades including the last one resulting in his disappearance.

[6] Koran 21 : 107.

[7] This may indicate that Ḥamzah, who was probably the one who drew this Charter, had a hand in the conspiracy that resulted in the murder of al-Ḥākim.

your prayer: "Behold our dwelling place!" And when the time comes for mercy to dawn upon you then shall the friend of Allah [al-Ḥākim] appear before you by his own accord, well satisfied with your conduct, visible in your midst.

Persist in the practice of these exercises, by day and by night, until the last day arrives, and the hour of judgment strikes, and the door of mercy is closed, and vengeance befalls all people of disobedience and disbelief. "He is fully excused who has amply forewarned,"[1] he has nothing to blame upon himself with regard to your case: he has given you full warning.

This is addressed to the people of intelligence among you; it is they who are particularly meant by it. It is the will of Allah (may he remain blessed and high!), and through him all success is achieved.

Peace be upon whomsoever follows guidance, fears the evil results of impiety, and believes in the excellent words of his Lord!

---

[1] A common Arabic saying.

Appendix D

EXCERPT FROM THE EPISTLE ENTITLED AL-QUSṬANṬĪNIYYAH ADDRESSED BY BAHĀ'-AL-DĪN TO THE BYZANTINE EMPEROR CONSTANTINE[1]

As for what you say in the special canticle for the Eucharist that "He suffered, was crucified in the time of Fayṭus, son of Qīlāṭūs,[2] was buried and arose on the third day," it is all recorded in the Gospel of John, chapter two, where Jesus addressing the Jews said to them: "Destroy the temple and I will raise it up in three days."[3] The Jews refused to believe his word that he would build the temple in three days. But what he meant was the temple of his body. And having mentioned [later] to his disciples what he had said they believed in the book[4] and in the word. Such is the text in the Gospel of John.

You should therefore know, you assembly of saints, that what he meant by the three days of his disappearance is firstly the day in which he declared his mission and called all mankind to the religion of Unity and truth[5] and revealed himself to the nations as a "true God from a true God." By that he meant that the Creator (may his power remain exalted!) is existent in his creatures, and that he manifests himself to them, as he has predetermined, in forms similar to their forms, and that he is

---

[1] Constantine VIII (1025–1028 A.D.).

[2] Pontius Pilate.

[3] *Cf.* John 2 : 19–22.

[4] Arabic *kitāb* referring to a book containing a revelation.

[5] Arabic *sidq*, always spelled in the Druze MSS. with a *sīn* instead of a *ṣād* so that the numerical value of the letters composing it may become 164, which is the number of the Druze ministers and missionaries.

not a nonentity so that it becomes necessary to use arguments to prove his existence to all his creation. Contemplate the truths of this assertion and beseech the Lord of guidance and might to accord you success.

As for the second day, that is the day of the appearance of the Paraclete.[1] Jesus has announced the Paraclete and predicted his coming, as Jesus has said in the Gospel of John: "Moses has written about me and predicted the mention of my name."[2] As for the Paraclete, he is Muḥammad, who is one of the legislators by whom I mean: Noah, Abraham, and Moses who appeared prior to the lord Messiah. And behold the saying of Jesus in the fifteenth chapter,[3] when he realized the coming of the Paraclete, *i.e.*, Muḥammad: "If you loved me you would rejoice at my departure to my Father, for my Father has a son who is greater than I. And now I have said this to you before it comes to pass, so when it comes to pass you shall believe in me." He did not say "believe in him." Then follows: "I shall not say many things to you, because the chief of this world shall come, and he has nothing in common with me. But this is so that people may know that I love my father."

The world withal never understood the meaning of his sayings. Jesus said that he [the Paraclete = Muḥammad] is the chief of this world only, and not of the next. This position, he—as well as the other legislators—attained, in fulfillment of the wisdom of the Creator, in order to have the case clear against mankind, one generation after another, and to render them subject to blame and condemnation; for they failed to follow what the Creator (may his power remain exalted!) had commanded them regarding the confession of Unity, which they forsook reverting by tradition to the worship of falsehood.

Referring to the Paraclete, Jesus said: "He has nothing in common with me." This is simply to inform you that he shall

---

[1] Arabic *fāraqlīṭ* = Comforter, Holy Ghost.

[2] *Cf.* John 5 : 46.

[3] It is in John 14 : 28–31.

not call mankind to a belief in the adorable Unity, as the Lord [Ḥamzah] shall call you to find the Creator in the Ḥākim-God, worthy of adoration.

As for the third day, it is the rise of al-Mahdi[1] (may Allah's blessing be upon him!) in order to call mankind to the inner interpretation of the four books which show the people of truth the fact of Unity. These four books are: the Psalter, the Torah [Bible], the Evangile and the Koran.

His [al-Mahdi's] epistles and proofs were received in their time by Constantine, the emperor of the Christians, and there is no doubt but that a record thereof is kept by the leading savants of that period, because his message differed from that of the other legislators who are weak; he having called people to the belief in the last day signalized by the appearance of the lord Messiah.

When, then, a man of understanding considers, and when a wise man, wishing to learn, removes the veil from a wide-awake, seeing and knowing heart, he would find out that al-Mahdi (may peace be upon him!) appeared and called to a belief in the inner interpretation of the aforementioned four books in the days of Constantine I, and that the lord Messiah [Ḥamzah] appeared calling to a belief in Unity in the days of Constantine II. People of intelligence would certainly find in this something to restrain them; and anyone possessed with the least notions of the science of truths would find material for reflection.

The third day is the complement of the first, according to the seventh chapter of the Gospel of John.[2] When the brothers of Jesus said to him: "Depart from here, so that your disciples may see the things you are doing, because no one should do a thing in secret, and reveal yourself to the world," the brothers of Jesus had not then believed in him. So Jesus said to them: "As for my time it has not arrived in realization," by which

---

[1] Sa'id al-Mahdi, one of the missionaries preceding al-Ḥākim.

[2] John 7 : 6.

he meant that his day was not yet completed. It is completed only when Jesus announces that he is ready to come again [into this world].

By his saying, "As for your time it is always ready," he meant to inform them that the time in which he was going to declare the word of Unity was not yet completed and had not yet come, but that their time—that is the time of those who did not know the word of Unity—was always ready. That is the last day which is the completion of the first. In it he [the lord Messiah] has manifested his glory and his praise and has shown himself to his apostles as he had promised them in chapter sixteen,[1] saying: "I have come down from heaven not to do my will, but the will of him who sent me. The will of him who sent me is that whosoever obeys me him will I resurrect on the last day; for this is the pleasure of my Father. For everyone who sees the son and believes in him is entitled to everlasting life which is fixed to the last day."

— — — — — — — — — — — — —

Written seven days before the end of Ṣafar, in the eleventh year of the era of the Ruler of the Age [Ḥamzah] at the end of the seventh year from the "disappearance [of al-Ḥākim] for our test."[2] This is the end; and praise be to our lord al-Ḥakim alone, and thanks to the Messiah of the nations [Ḥamzah] and their guide, his servant.

---

[1] John 6 : 38–40 and 47.

[2] Corresponding to March 23, 1028 A.D.

Appendix E

EXCERPT FROM BAHĀ'-AL-DĪN'S EPISTLE ENTITLED CHRISTIANITY

My trust I put in our lord the Ḥākim-God who is above number and child, and my thanks I offer to his servant, the only Messiah [Ḥamzah]. From the eloquent servant,[1] the slave of our lord the guide and Messiah, to all those who seek rapprochement to the deity through the reality of the Eucharist and who, of all people of truth, hold fast to the belief in it [*i.e.*, the Eucharist] be they priest, bishop or patriarch. Peace be upon the people who profess Unity, who walk in the footsteps of the holy apostles, who know the creed of the trusted, truthful saints whose souls are pure, who are steadfast in their loyalty to the Lord according to the covenant they made with him pledging their own souls, and who offer their lives in the love of the loyal one, the high priest, the martyr of martyrs, John the Evangelist, who sustained for the sake of his Lord insult, slaughter and beheadedness![2]

One of the strangest things of the age is how these people have forgotten the fundamentals of their religion, followed what has been forbidden them regarding loyalty to *Iblīs* and Satan, confessed by themselves the practice of what according to their own books of worship is false and untrue, agreed among themselves to follow evil and iniquity, and have become widely known among the people of truth, near and far, for their wicked beliefs.

---

1 *I.e.* Bahā'-al-Dīn, the writer of this epistle.

2 Bahā'-al-Dīn, who may have been a Christian apostate, confuses here John the Evangelist with John the Baptist, and in another place with John Chrysostom.

Where is then your loyalty to the Lord, O you assembly of hypocrites,[1] and where is your acceptance of his commandments, O liars, if you believe in him and trust in his return for the salvation of the people of truth from their sins? Did he not command you in the third chapter of the Gospel of Matthew saying: "Love your enemies, bless them who curse you, do good to them who do evil to you, pray for them who drive you away by force and chase you out haughtily and arrogantly; so that you may become children to your father who is in the heavens, who makes his sun to shine upon the good and the evil, and his rain to fall upon the righteous and the wicked? For if you love those who love you, what reward or credit should be given you? Even the Pharisees may do this very thing itself."[2]

O you stiff-necked and stupid ones, the remnant of idol worshipers! You have neither accepted him who gave you his commandment, recognized and remembered the one who announced to you beforehand his coming and directed his grace toward you, nor heard and obeyed his command.

O liars! You rather have violated the covenant of his command, you assembly of hypocrites, and disobeyed the word of the Lord who forbade you to obey satans. In this, you traitors, you have followed the example of the rebellious Jews who killed and scared the prophets. Likewise you have perpetrated evil and mischief against those who announced the coming of the lord Messiah, and practiced polytheism and real atheism which he forbade. You then persecuted the apostles and among them the learned one—the faithful and truthful sheikh—and in so doing you have deviated from the straight path, and forsaken the laws of the people of reality and of true religion, following the example of the priests and chiefs of the Jews in

---

[1] In the preceding Epistle to Constantine, Bahā'-al-Dīn addresses the Christians as "assembly of saints," because he was then still hopeful of winning them to the Druze religion.

[2] *Cf.* Matthew 5 : 44–47.

their dealing with the worshipful and kneeling Christians and in their rise to repel by unbelief and apostasy the word of the Lord after it had appeared.

Your case, you vicious ones, from the standpoint of deafness, imbecility and blindness, is similar to the case of a dumb animal, which, seeing by its side a man sympathizing with it because of some harm that has befallen it, gives him a painful kick that makes it impossible for him to administer the good he meant to administer to it. Such is your case, you who are too deaf to hear the truth and who refuse to accept the parables of the true Messiah.

Look, you heedless, but whence are you to get the right eye? And understand, but how are you to understand these parables extracted from the clear mines of truth? In the sixth chapter of the Gospel of Matthew, he said to the people: "Verily I say to you, the taxgatherers and hypocrites shall get into the kingdom of heaven before you, because John brought you the path of the Lord and of justice, and you did not believe him, although you saw him with your very eyes." You did not repent for what you had done, and did not believe in what you saw. You neither accepted the sermon of this clear wisdom nor respected the right of those who relate themselves to the Christian nation.

Appendix F

EXHORTATIONS AND PRAYERS BY AL-SAYYID 'ABDULLĀH AL-TANŪKHI[1]

I

EXHORTATION TO THE '*ĀQIL*[2]

It is incumbent upon the '*Āqil* that he should direct his energy only to the next world, preparing for it the provisions of piety, and not trusting this world which is a world of passage and not of settlement. He should begin with training his character, sensing its good qualities and purifying it from whatsoever alienates it from Allah (may he remain high!), such as bodily passion, greed for worldly possessions, anger, revenge, ill-temper, pride over others, and self-regard—all of which stand as a screen between him and the knowledge of his Creator (may he remain high!). And if he is thus screened from the knowledge of his Creator, he then becomes a victim to evil habits.

On the other hand, if the worshiper makes his chief ambition and desire the religion of Allah and the fear of him, holding fast to his commandments, abiding by his laws and turning his back upon what he has forbidden, then shall the Lord (may he remain high!) accord him success, bestow upon him his wisdom, and enlighten his heart rendering it like a polished mirror in which the divine facts are reflected. For wickedness, feebleness, evil whisperings and corruption lie dormant in the innermost part of

---

[1] Al-Sayyid 'Abdullāh, the last great commentator of the Druze religion, died in 1480 A.D.; and his tomb in 'Abayh, Lebanon, is annually visited by thousands of believers.

[2] Singular of '*Uqqāl* = enlightened, initiated, wise. See *supra*, p. 42.

the souls; and if the light of Unity and gnosis[1] should shine upon it, then all wickedness therein is destroyed, extinguished and exterminated—just as when the light of the sun shines, the light of the planets is eclipsed and entirely put out. Although the planets' light is extinguished in effect, yet it is in heaven in fact; but so long as the light of the sun is shining, the planets can produce no effect whatsoever. When the sun sets, however, then the planets will appear. Such is the case with the soul. As long as the light of reality and the knowledge of Allah (may he remain high!) are shining upon it, its darkness and its wickedness are dormant and have no trace; but in case wisdom and the knowledge of Allah (may he remain high!) set, then will evil qualities appear and reveal themselves in the same way as the stars reveal themselves when the sun sets.

Nothing, therefore, is more incumbent upon the *'Āqil* than to persevere in the religion of Allah, to abide by it day and night, and to bend every effort to keep the company of those who are useful and godly, so that they may add to his enlightenment. He should also imagine that Allah (may he remain high!) is with him, watching over him, and not departing from him for one wink of the eye. At all times should he be mentioning Allah's name, waiting upon him, and not neglecting him for one instant. He should fear no blame in the pursuit of truth, but should rather devote all energy and direct every sound mental power to the acquisition of the favor of the Lord of mankind, and the following of the path of right guidance which leads to victory on the last day.

II

COVENANT BETWEEN ALLAH AND SERVANT.

Said Allah: "O my servant, ten for thee and ten for me:— Be industrious and I shall give thee aid; demand, and I shall bestow; repent, and I shall forgive; thank, and I shall increase; depend, and I shall suffice; strive, and I shall give thee success;

---

[1] Arabic *ma'rifah* = knowledge.

beseech, and I shall respond; be content, and I shall enrich thee; ask and I shall give."[1]

III

PRAYER

O my God! Here is thy runaway slave returning to thy door, thy disobedient slave coming back for reconciliation, thy sinning slave bringing to thee his excuse. Pardon me by thy indulgence, accept me through thy bounty, and look unto me with thy mercy. O God! Forgive me my past iniquity, and guard me against committing iniquity in the remaining days of my life; for in thy hand is all good, and unto us thou are compassionate and merciful.

IV

PRAYER TO BE RECITED BEFORE SLEEP

In thy name, my Lord, I lay down my side; and in thy name, I lift it up. Protect me, O my God, against thy punishment on the day in which thou gatherest together thy creatures. In thy name, O Lord, I live and I die; and in thee I seek refuge against the evil of my own self, as well as against the evil of every creeping creature subject to thy control. Thou art the first: so before thee there is naught. Thou art the last: so after thee there is naught. O my Lord! Thou hast made my soul, and thou protectest it; thine is its death, and thine is its life. If thou, therefore, causest it to die, wilt thou pardon it; and if thou permittest it to live, wilt thou preserve it?

O my Lord! I beseech thee for health. I pray thee to awaken me at the hour that is most agreeable to thee, and to use me in the kind of work that is most acceptable to thee. Let thy grace draw me nigh unto thy favor, and alienate me from thy wrath. As I pray thee, grant my request; as I seek thy pardon, forgive me; and as I call upon thee, answer my prayer. "In the name of Allah, the merciful, the compassionate."

---

[1] This extract and the following prayers suggest Moslem Ṣūfi origin.

"Allah! There is no god but he, the living, the eternal. Slumber doth not seize him, nor sleep. His is whatsoever is in the heavens and whatsoever is in the earth. Who is he that can intercede with him but by his own permission? He knoweth what hath been before them and what shall be after them; yet naught of his knowledge shall they grasp, save what he willeth. His throne reacheth over the heavens and the earth, and the upholding of both burdeneth him not—and he is the high, the great!"[1]

---

[1] Koran 2 : 256.

INDEX

Aaron 37
'Abayh 9, 52
'Abd-al-Malik 22
'Abdullāh ibn-al-Mahdi 38
'Abdullāh al-Tanūkhi 52, 53, 71
Abraham 37, 65
Acre 15
Adam 36, 37, 39
al-Aghāni 42
Ajāwīd 42
'Ālayh 9, 52
Aleppo 3, 5, 10
'Ali 20, 27, 28, 30, 36, 37, 47
'Ali-Ilāhi 28
'Ali-Ilāhis 15, 53
Allah 40, 47, 48, 59–63, 71, 72, 74
American University of Beirūt 3
Antioch 3, 6, 10
'Āqil 71, 72
Arabia 8, 11, 21
Arabs 8, 14, 15, 17, 22, 23
Aramaisms 17
Arislāns 5, 22
Armenia 3, 15
Armenians 41
Asās (minor prophet) 37
Aṣḥāb al-Tanāsukh 45
al-Asrār, epistle 49
Assassins 3, 27
Assyria 1
ibn-al-Athīr 13, 23, 26
'Ayn-Dārah 8

Ba'aqlīn 6, 9
Babylonia 39
Baghdād 29
al-Baghdādi 28, 32, 40, 45
Bahā'-al-Dīn, al-Muqtana 11, 12, 20, 30, 34, 35, 38, 45, 49, 53, 68
Bahā'i 30
Bahā'is 48
Bahā'ism 30
Ba'labakk 22, 23
al-Balādhuri 22
al-Bār 20, 30, 57
Barham Amavand 32
Bar-Hebraeus 26
Bashan 2
Bashīr, al-Amīr 2, 7, 8
Bāṭiniyyah 19, 32, 36, 40
Bayṣūr 9
Beirūt 3, 5–7, 9
Bektāshis 15
Belfort (*Qal'at al-Shaqīf*) 2
Bell, Gertrude 14, 17
Benjamin of Tudela 13, 14, 47, 52
Bible 2, 31
Blavatsky, Madame 24
Blochet, E. 32
Brahman 46
"Brethren of Purity" (*Ikhwān al-Ṣafa*) 33, 35, 36
British 8, 15, 16
Browne, E. G. 41
Browning 31
Buddhism 41
Buddhist 41, 42

Cairo 1, 31
Casanova, Paul 49
China 46
Christ 1, 39

Christian 4
Christianity 3, 38, 39, 41, 48, 50, 68
Christians 8, 15, 29, 30, 70
Churchill, Col. 50
pseudo-Clementines 35
Commander of the Believers 59–62
Commandeurs du Liban 16
Conder, Lt.-Col. 50
Constantine I 66
Constantine II 66
Constantine VIII 11, 64, 66
Constantinople 6, 7, 9, 11
Copts 29
Crusaders 3, 6, 21
Crusades 2, 5
Cuthites 15
Cyrus 17

Damascus 5, 8, 9
Daniel 37
Darazi 12, 18, 19, 40, 50, 53, 54
Darazites 53, 54
Dayr-al-Qamar 9
Derusaiaioi 17
al-Dhahabi 11, 26
" Disappearance," *see ghaybah*
Dissimulation, *see taqiyyah*
Djevīd Bey 48
Docetae 39
Dog River 9
Domneh Jews 48
Dreux, comte de 15
Druids 16
Druze 46, 49
Druzes 1–3, 5, 6, 8–11, 13–18, 20–22, 24, 28–30, 38, 41, 45–49, 52–54
Druzes Réunis 16
Druzism 3, 4, 7, 18, 19, 22, 25, 27, 30, 39, 40, 41, 51
Dussaud 16

Edessa 2
Egypt 2, 6, 8, 11, 29
Elijah 31
Encyclopaedia Britannica 17
Encyclopaedia of Islam 13–14, 44, 54
Encyclopaedia of Religion and Ethics 35
Enoch 37
Esarhaddon 15
Essenes 39
Eucharist 64, 68
Evangile 66

Fakhr-al-Dīn ibn-Ma'n 2, 6, 7, 16, 21
Fāṭimite Caliphate 30
Fāṭimite dynasty 20
Fayṭus, son of Qilāṭūs 64
Ferdinand I 7, 16
abu-al-Fida 13, 26
al-Fihrist 39, 41
Florence 2
Florentines 7
France 16
Franks 2, 5, 6
Freemasonry 15
French 2, 15, 17, 44

Garrett, Robert 25
Genesis 39
Gharb 5
ghaybah (" disappearance ") 31, 67
Gibbon 27
God 29, 30, 33–36, 41, 47, 50, 64, 73
Godfrey of Bouillon 16
Gnostic 21
Gnosticism 35, 36, 41, 54
Gospel of John 64–66
Gospel of Matthew 69, 70
Goldziher, Ignacz 26, 29, 32, 42

al-Ḥā'iṭiyyah 45
halālīj, ihlīlīj 20
al-Ḥallāj 29
al-Ḥākim 11, 12, 18, 19, 25–31, 33, 34, 41, 46, 49, 50, 57–61
Ḥākim-God 26, 51, 66, 68

Ḥamāh 3
Ḥamzah 11, 12, 19, 20, 29, 34, 35, 40, 41, 44, 45, 49–53, 58
Ḥamzites 53, 54
Ḥārith ibn-Tarmāḥ 36
Ḥāṣbayya 9
d'Hautpoul, Beaufort 9
Ḥawrān 2, 6–10, 14
Ḥaydar, al-Amīr 21
ibn-Ḥazm 28, 40, 45
Herodotus 17
Ḥijāz 7, 8, 22
Ḥimṣ 3, 22
al-Ḥimyari, al-Sayyid 45
Hindoos 15
al-Ḥīrah 21, 22
Hiram, King 16
Hittites 15
Hivites 15
Holy Sepulchre 26
Ḥudūd (bounds, precepts) 34
Ḥujjah 37
al-Ḥulūliyyah 28
al-Ḥusayn ibn-Muḥammad 38

Iblīs (devil) 49, 51, 68
Ibrāhīm Pasha 2, 8, 25, 48
Ikhwān al-Ṣafa. See "Brethren of Unity"
'Imād 22
al-'Imādiyyah 22
Imām 31, 32, 58
Imāms 27, 37, 38, 59
India 3
Indian 32, 46
'Irāq 11, 19, 21, 22, 39
'Irāqi 33
Isaiah 31, 32
'Īsa ibn-Yūsuf. *See* Jesus
al-Isḥāqi 13
Ismā'īl ibn-Muḥammad 38
Ismā'īliyyah 3, 25, 27, 30–32, 37, 38, 40, 42
Islam 3, 6, 7, 25, 26, 28, 29, 39–42, 47, 48, 50, 52, 59
Ituraeans 14

al-Jabal al-A'la 9, 10
Jabal al-Durūz 6, 14
Jabriyyah 47
al-Jāḥiẓ 42
Janizaries 6
Japanese 14
ibn-al-Jawzi 45, 46
Jerusalem 26
Jesus ('Īsā ibn-Yūsuf) 37, 39, 64–67
Jews 15, 29, 64, 69
John the Evangelist 68
Judaeo-Christian sects 4, 29
Judaism 1, 24, 38
Juhhāl (uninitiate) 42
Jurjus al-Makīn 12, 26
Junblāṭs 22

Kafra 10
Kasrawān 6
al-Kaysāniyyah 45
ibn-Khaldūn 13, 29
khalwah (place of seclusion) 49
khalwahs 53
Khandy (Ceylon) 47
ibn-Khallikān 26
Khārijites 48
Khurāsān 11
Kitāb al-Naqḍ al-Khafi 40
Koran 25, 40, 47, 48, 66
Kurdish 21, 22
Kurdistān 3
Kurds 22

al-Laja 8
Lamaism 24
Lamartine 15, 16
Latin Kingdom 2
League of Nations 4
Lebanon 1–3, 5–11, 13–15, 17, 21, 44, 46, 49, 52, 53

anti-Lebanon 1
"Left Wing" ("Follower") 34
"Licensed" (*Ma'dhūn*) 36, 37
Logos 35
Lūristān 53
Luschan, Felix von 14, 15

Magian 39
Magians, *see Majūs*
Mahdi 31, 32, 66
Majūs (Magians) 23, 32, 46
al-Makīn. *See* Jurjus
Mamlūk Sultans 6
al-Ma'mūn, 33
Ma'n 5, 6
Mandaean 31
Mandaeanism 39
Mandaeans 46
Mani 39
Ma'ns 6, 7, 22
Manichaean 4, 21, 24, 39, 46, 50
Manichaeans 23, 39
Manichaeism 54
Manuscripts, Druze 11, 25, 28, 36, 39
al-Maqrīzi 45
Marcionite 38
Maronite 8, 48
Maronites 2, 15
al-Matn 9
Maundrell 16
al-Mawṣil 22
Mazdakian 46
Medicis 2
Mesopotamia 21
Messiah 29, 30, 32, 65–70
Michael the Paphlagonian 11
Moab 2
Montfort (*Qal'at Qurayn*) 2
Moses 29, 31, 37, 46, 65
Moslems 2, 59
Mt. Carmel 9, 10
Mt. Hermon 1, 2, 5, 7, 18
Mufawwaḍiyyah 36
Muḥammad ibn-'Abdullāh 38
Muḥammad 'Ali Pasha 8
Muḥammad ibn-Ismā'īl 37
Muḥammadiyyah 39
Muḥammad, the Prophet 7, 11, 36, 38, 50, 59, 65
al-Mukhtārah 9
al-Muqaṭṭam 31
al-Muqtana. *See* Bahā'-al-Dīn
Muṣṭafa Arislān 48
al-Mustarshid, Caliph 6
al-Mutawakkil 27
al-Mu'tazilah 33, 34
Muwaḥḥidūn. *See* Unitarians

Nāblus (Shechem) 1
Naples 7
Napoleon 2, 8
al-Nāṣir, al-Malik 6
Nāṭiq (legislating prophet) 37
Nazarenes 39
Near East 3, 11
Neo-Platonic 4, 32, 35, 41
Neo-Platonism 36, 41, 50, 54
New Testament 35, 39
Nicholson, R. A. 41
Niebuhr 14
Noah 37, 65
Nūr-al-Dīn, Sultan 6, 21
Nuṣayri 45, 52
Nuṣayriyyah 3, 15, 23, 28, 30, 36, 45, 53

"Opposer" (*Ḍudd*) 34–36
Oppenheim, von 14
Oriental Christian sects 4

Palestine 1, 9, 10, 15
Paraclete 65
Parfit, Canon 15
Persia 1, 3, 11, 19, 30, 33
Persian 18–23, 32, 33
Persians 15

Pharaoh 46
Pharisees 69
Philo 40
"Pioneer" (*Mukāsir* or *Naqīb*) 36, 37
Plato 37
Pococke 15–17, 49
Pompey 14
"Propagator" (*Dā'ī*) 36, 37
Psalter 66
Pythagorean 30, 38, 46

Qadarites 32, 47
Qadariyyah. *See* Qadarites
ibn-al-Qalānisi 26
al-Qarāmiṭah 27, 32, 35, 40, 42, 54
Qars (Ardaghān) 28
Qaysite 10
Qaysites 8
Quraysh 7

raj'ah ("return") 31, 33, 46
"Return," *see raj'ah*
"Right Wing" ("Precedent") 34
al-Rūdhrāwari 26

al-Saba'iyyah 28
Sacy, Silvestre de 25, 29, 49
Sadhus 42
Ṣafad 6, 9, 10
Saint-Pierre, Puget de 16
Saladin 7
Salonika 48
Samaritans 1, 15, 24
Ṣāmit ("silent") 37
Sargon 1
Sarraceni 13
Selīm I 6
al-Shahrastāni 28, 29, 40, 45, 46
al-Shalmaghāni 29
Sheikh 43
Sheikhs 42
Shibli al-'Aryān 8
al-Shidyāq 21
Shihāb 7
Shihābs 7
Shī'ah 23, 25, 27, 28, 30–33, 40, 47, 48, 54
Shī'ism 29
Shī'ite 4, 19, 26, 28, 32, 47, 48
al-Shūf 9
al-Shuwayfāt 9
Sidon 5, 6, 7, 47
Simon 37
Sitt-al-Mulk 31
Solomon's temple 16
Stavriote Greeks 48
Sublime Porte 2, 9
Ṣūfi 40, 41
Ṣūfis 42
Ṣūfism 41
Sulṭān Pasha al-Aṭrash 8
Ṣūr (Tyre) 22
al-Suyūṭi, 13
Syria 1–4, 6, 8–11, 13, 15, 17, 19, 21, 22, 44, 53
Syzygy 35

al-Ṭabari 21
Tadmur (Palmyra) 7
ibn-Taghri-Birdi 18
Ṭahtājis 15
Talḥūq 22
Tanūkhs 5, 21, 22
taqiyyah (dissimulation) 14, 22, 24, 47, 48
ibn-Taymiyyah 41
Templars 13
Theosphist, The 24
Torah 66
Tripoli 3, 6
Turks 2, 6, 48
Tuscany 7, 16

Unitarian 46, 57
Unitarians (*Muwaḥḥidūn*) 33, 34, 58

United States 10
" Universal Mind " 34
" Universal Soul " 34
'*Uqqāl* (initiate) 42

Vaux, Carra de 32
Vloten, van 29
Volney 16, 54

Wādi-al-Taym 1, 5, 7–10, 18, 19, 21, 23, 28, 44
Wahhābi 41
" Word," the 34, 35
Wali-al-Zamān 50, 57
Worsley, Mrs. 15

Yaḥya ibn-Sa'īd 12, 26
Yemenites 8, 10
Yezīdis 3, 15

Zaḥlah 9
zamān al-sitr (period of concealment) 25
Zenobia 7
Zindīq 42
Zoroastrian 4, 23, 32, 35
Zoroastrians 32

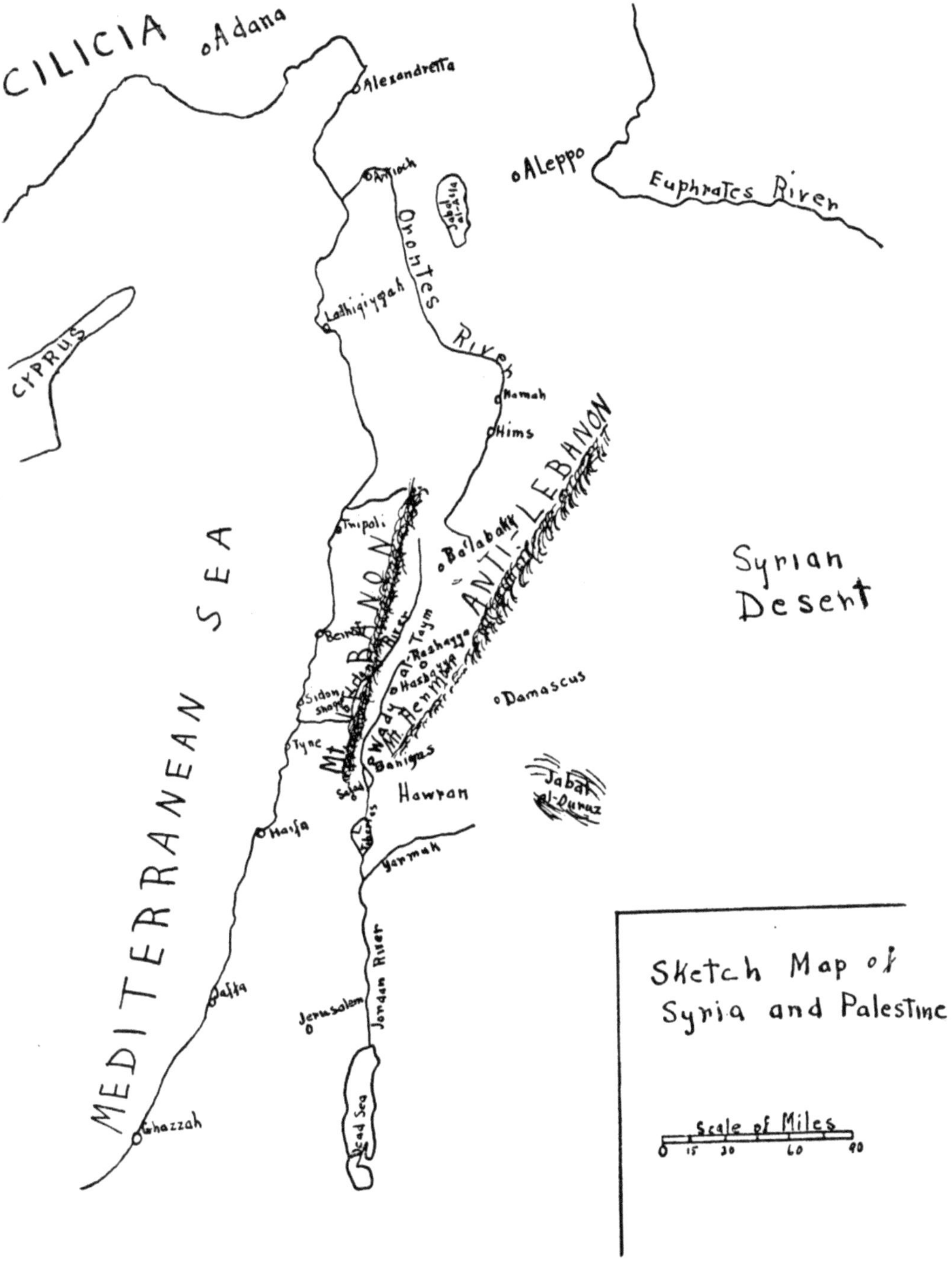

Sketch Map of
Syria and Palestine
Scale of Miles
0
15
30
60
90
CILICIA
Adana
Alexandretta
Antioch
Aleppo
Euphrates River
Orontes River
CYPRUS
Lathiqiyyah
Hamah
Hims
ANTI-LEBANON
Tripoli
Ba'labakk
Syrian Desert
MEDITERRANEAN SEA
Beirut
Sidon
Damascus
Tyre
Banias
Hawran
Jabal al-Duruz
Safad
Haifa
Yarmuk
Jordan River
Jaffa
Jerusalem
Dead Sea
Ghazzah

Bei Fragen zur Produktsicherheit wenden Sie sich bitte an:
If you have any questions regarding product safety,
please contact:

Walter de Gruyter GmbH
Genthiner Straße 13
10785 Berlin
productsafety@degruyterbrill.com